The Indian Today (annotated)

by Charles Eastman

BIOGRAPHICAL NOTE

The author of this book was born in a teepee of buffalo hide near Redwood Falls, Minn., during the winter of 1858. His father was a full-blooded Sioux called "Many Lightnings," (Tawakanhdeota). His mother, the granddaughter of Chief "Cloud Man" of the Sioux and daughter of a well-known army officer, died shortly after his birth. He was named Ohiyesa (The Winner).

The baby was reared to boyhood by the care of his grandmother. When he was four years old, the so-called "Minnesota massacre" of 1862 separated him from his father and elder brothers and only sister, and drove him with a remnant of the eastern Sioux into exile in Manitoba. There for over ten years he lived the original nomadic life of his people in the family of an uncle, from whom he received the Spartan training of an Indian youth of that day. The knowledge thus gained of life's realities and the secrets of nature, as well as of the idealistic philosophy of the Indian, he has always regarded as a most valuable part of his education.

When Ohiyesa had reached the age of fifteen years, and had been presented with a flint-lock musket in token of his arrival at the estate of young manhood, he was astonished by the reappearance of the father whose supposed death at the hands of white men he had been taught that he must some day avenge. He learned that this father had adopted the religion and customs of the hated race, and was come to take home his youngest son.

Ohiyesa's new home was a pioneer log cabin on a farm at Flandreau, Dakota Territory, where a small group of progressive Indians had taken up homesteads like white men and were earning an independent livelihood. His long hair was cropped, he was put into a suit of citizen's clothing and sent off to a mission day school. At first reluctant, he soon became interested, and two years later voluntarily walked 150 miles to attend a larger and better school at Santee, Neb., where he made rapid progress under the veteran missionary educator, Dr. Alfred L. Riggs, and was soon advanced to the preparatory department of Beloit College, Wisconsin. His father had adopted his wife's English name of Eastman, and the boy named himself Charles Alexander.

After two years at Beloit, young Eastman went on to Knox College, Ill.; then east to Kimball Union Academy in New Hampshire, and to Dartmouth College, where Indians had found a special welcome since colonial days. He was graduated from Dartmouth in 1887, and went immediately to Boston University, where he took the medical course, and was graduated in 1890 as orator of his class. The entire time spent in primary, preparatory, college, and professional education, including the mastery of the English language, was seventeen years, or about two years less than is required by the average white youth.

Doctor Eastman went directly to the large Pine Ridge reservation in South Dakota as Government physician; and during the "Ghost dance" troubles of 1890-91 he was in charge of the wounded Indian prisoners in their emergency hospital. In 1891 he married Miss Elaine Goodale of Berkshire County, Mass.; and in 1893 went to St. Paul, Minn., with his wife and child. While engaged there in the practice of medicine he was approached by a representative of the International Committee of the Y. M. C. A., and served for three years as their field secretary in the United States and Canada.

In 1897 Dr. Eastman went to Washington as attorney for his tribe, to push their interests at the national capital, and from 1899 to 1902 he served again as a Government physician to the Sioux. Beginning in 1903, he spent about seven years giving permanent family names to the Sioux, and thus helping to establish the legal descent of their property, under the direction of the Indian Bureau.

His first book, "Indian Boyhood," was published in 1902. It is the story of his own early life in the wilds of Canada, and was the outgrowth of several sketches which appeared in St. Nicholas a few years earlier. Since that time he has written "Red Hunters and the Animal People" (1904), "Old Indian Days" (1906), "Wigwam Evenings" (1909), "The Soul of the Indian" (1911), and "Indian Scout Talks" (1914). All have been successful, and some have been brought out in school editions, and translated into French, German, Danish, and Bohemian. He has also contributed numerous articles to magazines, reviews, and encyclopedias.

In connection with his writings he has been in steady demand as a lecturer and public speaker for the past twelve years, and has recently devoted his entire time to literary work and lecturing, with the purpose of interpreting his race to the present age.

When the first Universal Races Congress was held in the city of London in 1911, Dr. Eastman was chosen to represent the American Indian at that historic gathering. He is generally recognized as the foremost man of his race to-day, and as an authority on the history, customs, and traditions of the native Americans.

CONTENTS

CHAPTER

THE INDIAN TO-DAY

CHAPTER I

THE INDIAN AS HE WAS

It is the aim of this book to set forth the present status and outlook of the North American Indian. In one sense his is a "vanishing race." In another and an equally true sense it is a thoroughly progressive one, increasing in numbers and vitality, and awakening to the demands of a new life. It is time to ask: What is his national asset? What position does he fill in the body politic? What does he contribute, if anything, to the essential resources of the American nation?

In order to answer these questions, we ought, first, to consider fairly his native environment, temperament, training, and ability in his own lines, before he resigned himself to the inevitable and made up his mind to enter fully into membership in this great and composite nation. If we can see him as he was, we shall be the better able to see him as he is, and by the worth of his native excellence measure his contribution to the common stock.

In the first place, he is free born, hence a free thinker. His government is a pure democracy, based solidly upon intrinsic right and justice, which governs, in his conception, the play of life. I use the word "play" rather than a more pretentious term, as better expressing the trend of his philosophy. He stands naked and upright, both literally and symbolically, before his "Great Mystery." When he fails in obedience either to natural law (which is supreme law), or to the simple code of his brother man, he will not excuse himself upon a technicality or lie to save his miserable body. He comes to trial and punishment, even to death, if need be, unattended, and as cheerfully as to a council or feast.

As a free man himself, he allows others the same freedom. With him the spiritual life is paramount, and all material things are only means to the end of its ultimate perfection. Daily he meets the "Great Mystery" at morning and evening from the highest hilltop in the region of his home. His attitude toward Deity is simple and childlike.

Social life is kept as simple as possible, freedom of action only curbed by reverence for Those Above, and respect for the purity and perfection of his own body and those of his fellow-creatures. Only such laws are made as have been found necessary to guard personal and tribal purity and honor. The women do not associate freely with men outside of the family, and even within it strict decorum is observed between grown brothers and sisters. Birth and marriage are guarded with a peculiar sacredness as mysterious events. Strenuous out-of-door life and the discipline of war subdue the physical appetites of the men, and self-control is regarded as a religious duty. Among the Sioux it was originally held that children should not be born into a family oftener than once in three years, and no woman was expected to bear more than five children, for whom both masculine and feminine names were provided to indicate the order of their birth.

The Indian, in his simple philosophy, was careful to avoid a centralized population, wherein lies civilization's devil. He would not be forced to accept materialism as the basic principle of his life, but preferred to reduce existence to its simplest terms. His roving out-of-door life was more precarious, no doubt, than life reduced to a system, a mechanical routine; yet in his view it was and is infinitely happier. To be sure, this philosophy of his had its disadvantages and obvious defects, yet it was reasonably consistent with itself, which is more than can be said for our modern civilization. He knew that virtue is essential to the maintenance of physical excellence, and that strength, in the sense of endurance and vitality, underlies all genuine beauty. He was as a rule prepared to volunteer his services at any time in behalf of his fellows, at any cost of inconvenience and real hardship, and thus to grow in personality and soul-culture. Generous to the last mouthful of food, fearless of hunger, suffering, and death, he was surely something of a hero. Not "to have," but "to be," was his national motto.

As parents are responsible for the conduct of their children, so was the Indian clan responsible for the behavior of its members, both among themselves and in relation to other clans. This simple family government extended throughout the bands, tribes, and nations. There was no "politics" and no money in it for any one. The conscience was never at war with the mind, and no undue advantage was sought by any individual. Justice must be impartial; hence if the accused alone knew the facts, it was a common thing for him to surrender himself.

INTERTRIBAL WARFARE

As regards the original Indian warfare, it was founded upon the principle of manly rivalry in patriotism, bravery, and self-sacrifice. The willingness to risk life for the welfare or honor of the people was the highest test of character. In order that the reputations thus gained might be preserved as an example to the young, a system of decorations was evolved, including the symbolic wearing of certain feathers and skins, especially eagle feathers, and the conferring of "honor names" for special exploits. These distinctions could not be gained unjustly or by favoritism, as is often the case with rank and honors among civilized men, since the deeds claimed must be proved by witnesses before the grand council of war chiefs. If one strikes an enemy in battle, whether he kills him or not, he must announce the fact in a loud voice, so that it may be noted and remembered. The danger and difficulty is regarded above the amount of damage inflicted upon the enemy, and a man may wear the eagle plumes who has never taken a life.

It is easily seen that these intertribal contests were not based upon the same motives nor waged for the same objects as the wars of civilization-- namely, for spoil and territorial aggrandizement. There was no mass play; army was not pitted against army; individual valor was held in highest regard. It was not usual to take captives, except occasionally of women and children, who were adopted into the tribe and treated with kindness. There was no traffic in the labor or flesh of prisoners. Such warfare, in fact, was scarcely more than a series of duels or irregular skirmishes, engaged in by individuals and small groups, and in many cases was but little rougher than a game of university football. Some were killed because they were caught, or proved weaker and less athletic than their opponents. It was one way of disciplining a man and working off the superfluous energy that might otherwise lead to domestic quarrels. If he met his equal or superior and was slain, fighting bravely to the end, his friends might weep honorable tears.

The only atrocity of this early warfare was the taking of a small scalp lock by the leader, as a semi-religious trophy of the event; and as long as it was preserved, the Sioux warriors wore mourning for their dead enemy. Not all the tribes took scalps. It was only after the bounties offered by the colonial governments, notably in Massachusetts and Pennsylvania, for scalps of women and children as well as men, that the practice became general, and led to further mutilations, often stigmatized as "Indian," though in reality they have been practised by so-called civilized nations down to a recent period. That one should do murder for pay is not an Indian idea but one imposed upon the race by white barbarians.

It was a custom of the Plains Indians to hold peaceful meetings in summer, at which times they would vie with one another in friendliness and generosity. Each family would single out a family of another tribe as special guests of honor. Valuable horses and richly adorned garments were freely given at the feasts and dances. During these intertribal reunions the contests between the tribes were recalled and their events rehearsed, the dead heroes on both sides receiving special tributes of honor. Parents would entertain the participants in an engagement in which their son had fallen, perhaps, the year before, giving lavish hospitality and handsome presents in token that all was done in fair fight, and there remained no ill feeling.

FIRST EFFECTS OF CIVILIZATION

Whatever may be said for this scheme of life, its weaknesses are very apparent, and resulted in its early fall when confronted with the complicated system of our so-called civilization. With us the individual was supreme; all combination was voluntary in its nature; there was no commerce worthy the name, no national wealth, no taxation for the support of government, and the chiefs were merely natural leaders with much influence but little authority. The system worked well with men who were all of the same mind, but in the face of a powerful government and an organized army it quickly disintegrated and collapsed. Could the many small tribes and bands have formed a stable combination or league, they might have successfully resisted the invader; but instead they stood separately, though too weak to maintain their dignity by force, and in many cases entered upon a devastating warfare with one another, using the new and more deadly weapons, thus destroying one another. Since there was no central government, but a series of loose confederations of linguistic or allied groups, each of which had its titular head, able to make treaties or to declare war, these bands were met and subdued one at a time.

The original North American knew no fermented or spirituous drink. To be sure, he used a mild narcotic--tobacco mixed with aromatic leaves or bark, and smoked in strict moderation, generally as a semi-religious ceremony. Though wild grapes were found here in abundance, none had ever made wine from them. The introduction of liquor completed the ruin of our race.

During a long period the fur trade was an important factor in the world's commerce, and accordingly the friendship and favor of the natives were eagerly sought by the leading nations of Europe. Great use was made of whiskey and gunpowder as articles of trade. Demoralization was rapid. Many tribes were decimated and others wiped out entirely by the ravages of strong drink and disease, especially smallpox and cholera. The former was terribly fatal. The Indians knew nothing of its nature or treatment, and during the nineteenth century the tribes along the Mississippi and Missouri rivers suffered severely. Even in my own day I have seen and talked with the few desolate survivors of a thriving village.

In the decade following 1840 cholera ravaged the tribes dwelling along the great waterways. Venereal disease followed upon the frequent immoralities of white soldiers and frontiersmen. As soon as the Indian came into the reservation and adopted an indoor mode of life, bronchitis and pneumonia worked havoc with him, and that scourge of the present-day red man, tuberculosis, took its rise then in overcrowded log cabins and insanitary living, together with insufficient and often unwholesome food. During this period there was a rapid decline in the Indian population, leading to the now discredited theory that the race was necessarily "dying out" from contact with civilization.

It must always be borne in mind that the first effect of association with the more advanced race was not improvement but degeneracy. I have no wish to discredit the statements of the early explorers, including the Jesuit priests; but it is evident that in the zeal of the latter to gain honor for their society for saving the souls of the natives it was almost necessary to represent them as godless and murderous savages--otherwise there would be no one to convert! Of course they were not angels, but I think I have made it clear that they were a God-fearing, clean, and honorable people before the coming of the white man.

THE TRANSITION PERIOD

The transition from their natural life to the artificial life of civilization has been very gradual in most cases, until the last fifty years, when the changes have been more rapid. Those who were first affected were the so-called "Five Civilized Nations" of the South, and the "Six Nations" of New York State, together with some of the now extinct bands in New England, who came in close touch with the early colonists. Both politically and commercially, they played an important part in the settlement of America. Their services as scouts, guides, and allies were of great value in the early history of this country, and down to recent years. Many received no salary, and some even furnished their own horses. It is a remarkable fact that there is not one instance on record of a scout betraying the cause he served, even though used against his own tribe and his own relatives. Once his honor is pledged to a public trust, he must sustain it at any cost.

In many cases those tribes which declared allegiance to the French, the English, or the Americans, were in their turn the means of bringing a neighboring tribe into subjection. Thus began a new era in the history of the Indian, inaugurating a kind of warfare that was cruel, relentless, and demoralizing, since it was based upon the desire to conquer and to despoil the conquered of his possessions--a motive unknown to the primitive American.

To be sure the new weapons were more efficient, and therefore more deadly; the new clothing was gayer, but less perfectly adapted to the purposes of primitive life. Indeed, the buckskin clothing and moccasins of the Indian were very generally adopted by the white frontiersman. On the other hand, his spiritual and moral loss was great. He who listened to the preaching of the missionaries came to believe that the white man alone has a real God, and that the things he had hitherto held sacred are inventions of the devil. This undermined the foundations of his philosophy, and very often without substituting for it the Christian philosophy, which the inconsistency of its advocates, rather than any innate quality, made it difficult for him to accept or understand.

A few did, in good faith, accept the white man's God. The black-robed preacher was like the Indian himself in seeking no soft things, and as he followed the fortunes of the tribes in the wilderness, the tribesmen learned to trust and to love him. Then came other missionaries who had houses to sleep in, and gardens planted, and who hesitated to sleep in the Indian's wigwam or eat of his wild meat, but for the most part held themselves aloof and urged their own dress and ways upon their converts. These, too, had their following in due time. But in the main it is true that while the Indian eagerly sought guns and gunpowder, knives and whiskey, a few articles of dress, and, later, horses, he did not of himself desire the white man's food, his houses, his books, his government, or his religion.

The two great "civilizers," after all, were whiskey and gunpowder, and from the hour the red man accepted these he had in reality sold his birthright, and all unconsciously consented to his own ruin. Immediately his manhood began to crumble. A few chiefs undertook to copy some of the European ways, on the strength of treaty recognition. The medals and parchments received at such times were handed down from father to son, and the sons often disputed as to who should succeed the father, ignoring the rule of seniority and refusing to submit to the election of the council. There were instances during the nineteenth century in the vicinity of Chicago, Prairie du Chien, Saint Paul, and Kansas City, where several brothers quarrelled and were in turn murdered in drunken rows. There was also trouble when the United States undertook to appoint a head chief without the consent of the tribe. Chief Hole-in-the-Day of the Ojibways and Spotted Tail of the Brule Sioux were both killed by tribesmen for breaking the rule of their respective tribes and accepting favors from the Government.

Intermarriages were not common among the different tribes in the old days, and still less so between Indians and Caucasians. The earlier intermarriages were with the higher class of Europeans: officers, noblemen, etc., and many of the offspring of these unions were highly esteemed, some becoming chiefs. At this period the natives preferred their own marriage customs, which was convenient for the white officers who were thus enabled to desert their wives and children when they chose, and often did so, quite as if there were no binding obligation. Later, when unions between the lower class of both races became common, the Sioux refused to recognize their half-breeds as members of the tribe, and a certain territory was set apart for them. These half-breeds disposed of their land to the Government, and took instead certificates entitling them to locate upon the public domain. Some thirty years afterward they returned to their mother tribe and were allowed full rights as members of their respective bands.

Except among the French Canadians, in no section has there been such a general intermingling of the blood of the two races as in the Southern States. The Virginia legislature early recognized intermarriages between whites and Indians, and from the time of Pocahontas to this day some of the best families have married among Cherokees, Chickasaws, and Choctaws, and are proud of the infusion of aboriginal blood. Among the "Five Civilized Tribes" of Oklahoma the Indian blood is distinguishable only in a minority of those who call themselves "Indians."

This transition period has been a time of stress and suffering for my people. Once they had departed from the broad democracy and pure idealism of their prime, and undertaken to enter upon the world-game of competition, their rudder was unshipped, their compass lost, and the whirlwind and tempest of materialism and love of conquest tossed them to and fro like leaves in the wind.

"You are a child," said the white man in effect to the simple and credulous native. "You cannot make or invent anything. We have the only God, and he has given us authority to teach and to govern all the peoples of the earth. In proof of this we have His Book, a supernatural guide, every word of which is true and binding. We are a superior race--a chosen people. We have a heaven fenced in with golden gates from all pagans and unbelievers, and a hell where the souls of such are tortured eternally. We are honorable, truthful, refined, religious, peaceful; we hate cruelty and injustice; our business is to educate, Christianize, and protect the rights and property of the weak and the uncivilized."

This sort of talk had its effect. Let us see what followed.

CHAPTER II

THE HOW AND THE WHY OF INDIAN WARS

I have tried to set forth the character and motives of the primitive Indian as they were affected by contact with civilization. In a word, demoralization was gradual but certain, culminating in the final loss of his freedom and confinement to the reservation under most depressing conditions. It must be borne in mind that there has been scarcely any genuine wild life among us for the past thirty-five years. Sitting Bull's band of Sioux were the last real hostiles of their tribe to surrender, in 1880, and Geronimo's Apaches followed in 1886.

It is important to understand the underlying causes of Indian wars. There are people to-day who believe that the Indian likes nothing better than going on the warpath, killing and scalping from sheer native cruelty and lust for blood. His character as a man of peace has not been appreciated. Yet it is matter of history that the newcomers were welcomed in almost every case with unsuspecting kindness, and in his dealings with the white man the original owner of the soil has been uniformly patient and reasonable, offering resistance only under irresistible provocation.

There have been but few noteworthy Indian wars in the history of America. In 1629 Powhatan's brother revolted against the colonists in Virginia, and King Philip took up arms in Massachusetts in 1675. The Cherokee war of 1758 in North and South Carolina came next; then the conspiracy of Pontiac in 1763, the Creek war from 1812 to 1830, and the Seminole war from 1820 to 1833. These wars in the South were incited by the insolence and aggressiveness of the Americans. The struggles of the Algonquins and the Iroquois, however, were not conducted wholly on their own initiative. These tribes were used as allies in the long-drawn-out conflicts between the French and the English, and thus initiated into the motives and the methods of the white man's warfare.

I doubt very much if Pontiac would have carried his policies so far had it not been for the encouragement he received from French traders and settlers, who assured him that King Louis would come to his assistance in due time, with men and ammunition. Strong in this belief, as well as in his innate sense of right and justice, he planned to unite the scattered tribes against the invader and overthrow all the border forts in a day. His boldness and aggressiveness were unique in the history of Indian warfare.

At this juncture a remarkable man was chosen to guide the Indian policy in America. Sir William Johnson had long been engaged in trade among the Six Nations, and more especially the Mohawks. His influence among them was very great; and it was partly through his conciliatory methods, and partly by reason of the betrayal of his plans and the failure of the French to keep their promises of assistance, that Pontiac, perhaps our greatest military genius, was forced to surrender.

A sad feature of the early wars was the sufferings of those Indians who had listened to the preaching of Jesus Christ. In Massachusetts, during King Philip's war, the Christian Indians were treated no better than the "heathen savages." Some were hanged, some imprisoned, and some sold as slaves to the West Indies. At best, they lost their homes and improvements, and nearly perished of cold and hunger. In Pennsylvania, at Conestoga and Wyoming Valley, they were horribly murdered, and the peaceful Moravian Indians were butchered at prayer in their church, while no one dared say a word of protest except the Quakers.

To return to the wars in the South, many of these were mere feuds between one or two families. The Cherokees secured concessions and promises of better treatment from the white men, after which they continued friendly, and helped in overcoming the Creeks and Seminoles.

Practically all Indian wars have been caused by a few self-seeking men. For instance, a man may secure through political influence a license to trade among the Indians. By his unprincipled practices, often in defiance of treaty agreements, such as gross overcharging and the use of liquor to debauch the natives, he accumulates much tainted wealth. This he invests in lands on the border or even within the Indian territory if ill-defined. Having established himself, he buys much stock, or perhaps sets up a mill on Indian water-power. He gathers his family and hirelings about him, and presently becomes a man of influence in his home state. From the vantage point of a rough border town, peopled largely with gamblers, saloonkeepers, and horse-thieves, this man and his kind plot the removal of the Indian from his fertile acres. They harass him in every way, and having at last forced resistance upon him, they loudly cry: "Indian outbreak! Send us troops! Annihilate the savages!"

OSCEOLA AND THE SEMINOLES

The principal causes of Indian troubles in the South were, first, the encroachments of this class of settlers; second, the hospitable willingness of the Indians to shelter fugitive slaves. Many of these people had found an Elysium among the Creeks and Seminoles, and had even intermarried among them, their offspring becoming members of the tribe. Osceola's wife was of this class--a beautiful Indian woman with some negro and some white blood. She was dragged away from him by unholy traffickers in human flesh, and he was arrested for remonstrating. Who could tolerate such an outrage? The great chief was then a young man and comparatively unknown; but within one year he became the recognized leader of his tribe and the champion of their cause. The country was perfectly suited to the guerilla warfare which is characteristic of Indians--a country in which even an Indian of another tribe would be lost! White frontiersmen were imported to guide the army, but according to the testimony of Beckworth, the Rocky Mountain hunter and trapper, all gave up in disgust. The Government was forced to resort to pacific measures in order to get the Seminoles in its power, and eventually most of them were removed to the Indian Territory. There was one small band which persistently refused the offered terms, and still remains in the fastnesses of the Florida Everglades, perhaps the only unconquered band in the United States to-day.

While the Southern tribes were deported almost in a body to what was then the far West, the wars of the Algonquins, along the Great Lakes and the Ohio River, scattered them far and wide in fragments. Such of the Iroquois as had strong treaties with the Dutch colony secured permanent reservations in the State of New York which they still occupy, having been continuously under state control instead of that of the general government.

CHIEF JOSEPH'S REASONING

The Black Hawk war in 1836 was the end of the Algonquin resistance. Surely if there was ever just cause for resistance, Black Hawk had such a cause. His case was exactly similar to that of the famous Nez Perce, Chief Joseph, who illustrates his grievance very lucidly in the North American Review for April, 1879, in an interview with Bishop Hare of South Dakota.

"If I ever sold any land to the Government," says he, "it was done in this way: Suppose a man comes to me and says: 'Joseph, I want to buy your horse.' I say to him: 'I am satisfied with my horse. I do not wish to sell him at any price.' Then the man goes to my neighbor and says to him: 'I want to buy

Joseph's horse, but he would not sell it to me.' My neighbor says: 'If you will buy my horse, I will throw in his horse!' The man buys my neighbor's horse, and then he comes and claims my horse and takes it away. I am under no obligation to my neighbor. He had nothing to do with my horse."

It was just such dealing as this which forced Black Hawk to fight with a handful of warriors for his inheritance. The Government simply made a treaty with the Sacs under Keokuk, and took the land of the Foxes at the same time. There were some chiefs who, after they had feasted well and drunk deep and signed away their country for nothing, talked of war, and urged Black Hawk to lead them. Then they sneaked away to play "good Indian," and left him to bear the brunt alone.

There were no more Indian wars for thirty years. The Southwest frontiers were now occupied by eastern tribes or their remnants, which had been transported beyond the Mississippi during the early thirties. Only fragments were left here and there, in New York, Pennsylvania, Ohio, Indiana, and the South. The great Siouan race occupied nearly all the upper valley of the Mississippi and Missouri rivers and their tributaries. North of them dwelt the Ojibways, an Algonquin tribe with an entirely different language. The Sioux nation proper originally occupied a vast territory, and in the middle of the nineteenth century they still held the southern half of Minnesota, a portion of Wisconsin and Iowa, all of the Dakotas, part of Montana, nearly half of Nebraska, and small portions of Colorado and Wyoming. Some of the bands were forest Indians, hunters and trappers and fishermen, while others roamed over the Great Plains and hunted the buffalo, elk, and antelope. Some divided the year between the forest and prairie life. These people had been at peace with the whites ever since the early French explorers and the Jesuit priests had entered their country. They had traded for many years with the Hudson Bay and American Fur companies, and no serious difficulty had arisen, nor was any obstruction offered to the progress of civilization.

In 1824 the United States required of the tribes in this region to define their territory, a demand which intensified and gave a new turn to their intertribal warfare. The use of gun, horse, and whiskey completed the demoralization, and thus the truly "savage" warfare had its origin, ever increasing in bitterness until it culminated in resistance to the Government, in 1862, one hundred years after the struggle and defeat of the great Pontiac.

THE SIOUX AND THEIR GRIEVANCES

A treaty was made in 1851 with the Minnesota Sioux to which one band was not a party. This was the one commonly known as Inkpaduta's band, whose usual winter resort was in northwestern Iowa. White settlers went upon the ceded lands, and when this band returned to Spirit Lake after their summer's roving they found it occupied. Owing to a very severe winter and the presence of the settlements, the surrounding country became depleted of game, and the Sioux, who were starving, sought aid among the settlers. No doubt they became a nuisance, and were so treated, which treatment they very naturally resented, and thus arose the "Spirit Lake massacre." The rest of the tribe condemned the act, and Sioux from the Redwood reservation pursued the guilty band until they overtook and killed two of Inkpaduta's sons. The others were driven back among the wild Sioux. This was their first offence, after more than a century of contact with the whites.

Little Crow's band formed the east wing of the Sioux nation, and were the first to enter reservation life. The causes of their outbreak, a few years later, were practically the same as in many other instances, for in its broad features the history of one Indian tribe is the history of all. Their hunting-grounds were taken from them, and the promised support was not forthcoming. Some of the chiefs began to "play politics" like white men, and through their signatures, secretly given, a payment of $98,000 due the tribe was made to the Indian traders. Little Crow himself was involved in this steal, and was made head chief by the whites, who wished to have some one in this position whom they could deal with. But soon the non-payment of annuities brought the Indians to the verge of starvation, and in despair they forced Little Crow to lead them in revolt. In August, 1862, they massacred the agency employees and extended their attack to the white settlers, killing many and destroying a large amount of property, before a part of the tribe fled into Canada and the rest surrendered to General Sibley.

Next came the struggle of the Western Sioux and Northern Cheyennes in defence of their homes. The building of the Northern Pacific and the Union Pacific transcontinental railroads had necessitated the making of new treaties with these people. Scarcely was the agreement completed by which they ceded a right of way in return for assurances of permanent and absolute possession of other territory, including the Black Hills and Bighorn Mountains, when gold was discovered in these regions. This fact created great excitement and a general determination to dispossess the Sioux of the country just guaranteed to them, which no white man was to enter without the consent of three fourths of the adult men of the tribe.

Public excitement was intense, and the Government found itself unable to clear the country of intruders and to protect the rights of the Sioux. It was reported that there were no less than fifteen thousand men in the Black Hills district placer-mining and prospecting for the yellow metal. The authority of the United States was defied almost openly by the frontier press and people. Then the Indians took matters into their own hands, carried on a guerilla warfare against immigrants, and harassed the forts until the army was forced to enter upon a campaign against them. In 1868 another treaty was made, but the great chief, Red Cloud, would not sign it until he saw forts C. F. Smith and Phil Kearney abandoned. Here is probably the only instance in American history in which a single Indian chief was able to enforce his demands and make a great government back down. At that time it would have cost immense sums of money and many lives to conquer him, and would have retarded the development of the West by many years.

It is a fact that Sitting Bull was thoroughly opposed to yielding any more territory. No doubt he foresaw the inevitable result. He had taken up the cause of the Eastern Sioux in Minnesota and fought Sibley and Sully in 1862. He had supported Red Cloud in his protests against the establishment of the Bozeman trail, and against the new forts, although thus far these aggressions had not affected him directly. But when surveyors began work on the Northern Pacific, they entered his particular domain, and it was time for him to fight in its defence. Unfortunately for him, the other bands of Sioux whom he had helped in their time of need were now all settled upon reservations, so that he had not much support except from Crazy Horse's band, and the so-called hostiles or renegades of the Western bands. Hostilities began in 1872, culminating in 1876 with the famous "Custer fight," which practically ended the struggle, for after annihilating Custer's command the Indians fled into British America. Four years later Sitting Bull was induced to come in and settle down upon the Sioux reservation.

The Modoc war in Oregon and Idaho, in which the Shoshones and Bannocks were involved, was really a part of this same movement--namely, the last defence of their hunting-grounds by the Plains Indians, as was also the resistance of the Cheyennes and Comanches farther south, and of the Utes in 1877, simultaneously with the last stand of the Sioux. It had been found impossible to conquer the Plains Indians without destroying the buffalo, their main subsistence. Therefore vast herds were ruthlessly destroyed by the United States army, and by 1880 they were practically extinct. Since it was found cheaper to feed than to fight them, the one-time warriors were corralled upon their reservations and kept alive upon Government rations.

THE "GHOST-DANCE WAR"

All Indian warfare worthy the name had now come to an end. There were left Geronimo's small bands of Apaches, who were hunted down in an all but inaccessible country and finally captured and confined in Southern forts. More recent "Indian outbreaks," so-called, are usually a mere ruse of the politicians, or are riots caused by the disaffection of a few Indians unjustly treated by their Government agents. The only really serious disturbance within a generation was the "Ghost-dance war" of 1890-91. And yet this cannot fairly be called an Indian war. It arose in a religious craze which need not have been a serious matter if wisely handled. The people were hungry and disheartened, their future looked hopeless, and all their appeals were disregarded. At this juncture the suggestion of a Messiah, offering hope of miraculous intervention in behalf of the red man, appealed to many, and the "new religion" spread far and fast. In some tribes it soon died a natural death, but in the Sioux country it was unwisely forbidden by the authorities, and led to grave results.

At Pine Ridge, in December of 1890, the ghost-dancers had come in to the agency and the situation was apparently under control when the attempted arrest of Sitting Bull in his cabin by Indian police led to his death and the stampeding of his people. Several of the stampeded bands came down to Pine Ridge, where they were met by United States troops, disarmed, and shot down after one man had resisted disarmament by firing off his weapon. This was the massacre of Wounded Knee, where about 300 Indians, two thirds of them women and children, were mown down with machine-guns within a few minutes. For some days there was danger of a reprisal, but the crisis passed, and those Indians who had fled to the "Bad Lands" were induced to come in and surrender. From that time on the Indian tribes of the United States have been on a peace footing.

CHAPTER III

THE AGENCY SYSTEM: ITS USES AND ABUSES

The early colonists, accustomed to European usages, undertook to deal with a native chief as if he were a king, with the power to enforce his rule over his people. As a matter of fact, he was merely their spokesman, without authority except as it was given him by the council of his clan, which was called together in any important event. Each clan or band was responsible only for its own members, and had nothing to do with the conduct of any other band. This difference of viewpoint has led to serious trouble.

TREATIES AND TRUST FUNDS

Most of the early agreements were merely declarations of peace and friendship, allowing freedom of trade, but having nothing to do with any cession of land. In New England small tracts of land were purchased by the settlers of individual Indians who happened to sojourn there for the time being, and purchased for a nominal price, according to their own history and records. The natives had no conception of ownership in the soil, and would barter away a princely estate for a few strings of beads or a gallon of rum, not realizing that they conveyed the absolute and exclusive title that they themselves, as individuals, had not pretended to possess.

The status of the Indians within the United States has been repeatedly changed since colonial times. When this Government was founded, while claiming the right of eminent domain over the whole country, it never denied the "right of occupancy" of the aborigines. In the articles of confederation Congress was given sole power to deal with them, but by the constitution this power was transferred in part to the executive branch. Formal treaties were made which had to be ratified by the Senate, until in 1871 Congress declared that the Indian tribes might no longer be recognized as independent nations, and reduced the treaties to simple "agreements," which, however, must in ethics be considered fully as binding. Their natural resources had now in many cases been taken from them, rendering them helpless and dependent, and for this reason some of the later treaties provided that they should be supported until they became self-supporting.

In less than a century 370 distinct treaties were made with the various tribes, some of them merely friendship agreements, but in the main providing for right of way and the cession of lands, as fast as such lands were demanded by the westward growth of the country and the pressure of population. In the first instance, the consideration was generally not over five or ten cents an acre. While the Indians were still nomadic in their habits, goods in payment were usually taken by steamboat to the nearest point and there turned over to the head chiefs, who distributed them among the people. Later the price increased and payments were made either in goods or cash; fifty cents to a dollar and a quarter, and more recently as much as $2.50 per acre for cessions of surplus lands on reservations after the owners have all been allotted. Gradually large trust funds have been created for some of the tribes, the capital being held in the United States Treasury and the interest paid to the Indians in annual per capita instalments, or expended "for their benefit." Farmers, blacksmiths, carpenters, and other industrial teachers; cattle, farming tools, houses, and schools are variously promised in the later treaties for the "support and civilization" of a people whose own method of making a living has been rendered forever impossible. The theory was humane and just, but the working of the system has proved in a large degree a failure.

WHAT ARE RESERVATIONS?

A natural result of frequent land cessions was the reserving or setting aside of tracts of land for Indian occupancy, known as "reservations." Such lands have been set aside not only by treaty but in many cases by act of Congress, and in others by executive order. The Indians living upon them may not sell standing timber, or mining rights, or right of way to railroads, without the consent of the Government.

The policy of removal and concentration of Indians originated early in the nineteenth century, and was carried partially into effect. Indian Territory was set apart as a permanent home for the tribes, and the Creeks, Cherokees, Choctaws, Chickasaws, and Seminoles were removed thither from the Southeastern States. After a terrible journey, in which many died of disease and exhaustion, and one boatload sank in the Mississippi River, those who were left established themselves in the "Promised Land," a country rich in natural resources. They soon saw the necessity of a stable government and of domestic and agricultural pursuits. They copied the form of their government after that of the States, and the trust funds arising from the sale of their eastern lands formed the basis of their finances. They founded churches, schools, and orphan asylums, and upon the whole succeeded remarkably well in their undertaking, although their policy of admitting intermarried whites and negroes to citizenship in the tribe led to much political corruption. Gradually some forty tribes, or tribal remnants, were colonized in the Territory; but this scheme failed in many instances, as some tribes (such as the Sioux) refused absolutely to go there, and others who went suffered severely from the change of climate. In 1890 the western part was made into a separate territory under the name of Oklahoma and colonized by whites; and in 1907 the entire territory was admitted to statehood under that name, the "Five Civilized Nations," so-called, having been induced to give up their tribal governments.

The Indians of the Southwest came in, in 1848, under the treaty of Guadalupe Hidalgo, although with some of them other treaties have been made and their lands added to by executive order. The Navajoes, about twenty-two thousand in number, now own more than twelve million acres in Arizona and New Mexico. They are sheep-herders and blanket-weavers, and are entirely self-supporting. Owing to the character of the land they occupy, and the absence of sufficient water for irrigation, there is not enough grass on the reservation to support all the Indian stock. Therefore 5,000 or more Navajoes are living outside the reservation, on the public domain; and of these, according to Indian Office statements, about 1,000 are unallotted, and under the present law can only be allotted as are white homesteaders, by paying the costs of survey and fees to the land office.

The Pueblos hold their lands (about 1,000,000 acres) under Spanish grants, and are in absolute control of them, so that the Government cannot build schoolhouses among them unless sites are deeded for that purpose, which they are sometimes unwilling to do. These people are still self-governing, but their titles are now in danger, owing to a recent ruling of the local courts that declares them citizens, and as such liable to taxation. Being for the most part very poor and fearing to have their land sold for taxes, they have petitioned the United States to act as trustee to manage their estates.

The natives of California were a peaceable people and made scarcely any resistance to the invaders, a fact which has resulted in their rapid decline and extreme poverty. Under the Spanish friars they were gathered into missions and given a general industrial training, but after the secularization of the missions the Americans took possession of their cultivated lands, and many of the Indians were landless and homeless. The remnants are now living as squatters upon the property of white settlers, or on small pieces of land allotted them by the Government.

In striking contrast to the poverty-stricken condition of these Pacific Coast Indians is the wealth of the Osages, a small Siouan tribe occupying a fertile country in Oklahoma, who are said to be the richest people, per capita, in the world. Besides an abundance of land, rich in oil and timber, they have a trust fund of eight million dollars in the United States Treasury, bringing in a large annual income. They own comfortable houses, dwell in substantial towns, and are moderately progressive.

THE TRUTH ABOUT INDIAN AGENCIES

The Indian of the Northwest came into reservation life reluctantly, very much like a man who has dissipated his large inheritance and is driven out by foreclosure. One morning he awoke to the fact that he must give up his freedom and resign his vast possessions to live in a squalid cabin in the backyard of civilization. For the first time his rovings were checked by well-defined boundaries, and he could not hunt or visit neighboring tribes without a passport. He was practically a prisoner, to be fed and treated as such; and what resources were left him must be controlled by the Indian Bureau through its resident agent.

Who is this Indian agent, or superintendent, as he is now called? He is the supreme ruler on the reservation, responsible directly to the Commissioner of Indian Affairs; and all requests or complaints must pass through his office. The agency doctor, clerks, farmers, superintendents of agency schools, and all other local employees report to him and are subject to his orders. Too often he has been nothing more than a ward politician of the commonest stamp, whose main purpose is to get all that is coming to him. His salary is small, but there are endless opportunities for graft.

If any appeal from the agent's decisions, they are "kickers" and "insubordinate." If they are Indians, he can easily deprive them of privileges, or even imprison them on trumped-up charges; if employees, he will force them to resign or apply for transfers; and even the missionaries may be compelled, directly or indirectly, to leave the reservation for protesting too openly against official wrongdoing. The inspector sent from Washington to investigate finds it easy to "get in with" the agent and very difficult to see or hear anything that the agent does not wish him to hear or see. Many Indians now believe sincerely in Christ's teachings as explained to them by their missionaries, but they find it impossible to believe that this Government is Christian, or the average official an honest man.

Any untutored people, however, are apt imitators, and so these much-exploited natives become politicians in spite of themselves. The most worthless of the tribe are used as the agent's spies and henchmen; a state of affairs demoralizing on the face of it. As long as the Indian Bureau is run in the interests of the politicians, and Indian civilization is merely an incident, the excellent and humanitarian policies approved by the American people will not be fully carried into effect.

It is true that good men and especially good women have gone into the Indian service with a genuine desire to deal justly and kindly by the Indian and to serve the Government honorably and efficiently. Such people often become disgusted with the system and find it impossible to stay, or else are forced out by methods familiar to the experienced. When you clear your American cities of grafters, and purify your politics, then perhaps you will be in a position to redeem the Indian service, and only then. Alas! the skirts of the Goddess of Liberty have never yet been quite clean!

The Indian is no fool; on the other hand, he is a keen observer and an apt student. Although an idealist by nature, many of the race have proved themselves good business men. But under the reservation system they have developed traits that are absolutely opposed to the racial type. They become time-serving, beggarly, and apathetic. Some of their finest characters, such as Chief Joseph, have really died of a broken heart. These are men who could not submit to be degraded; the politicians call them "incorrigible savages."

The distribution of rations to the Plains Indians was, as I have explained, originally a peace measure, and apparently a necessity in place of their buffalo which the white man had exterminated. For many years Texas beef was issued monthly "on the hoof"; that is, the cattle were driven out one by one upon the plain, and there surrounded and shot down by representatives of the groups to which they belonged. Bacon, flour, sugar, and coffee were doled out to the women, usually as often as once in two weeks, thus requiring those who lived at a considerable distance from the agency to spend several days of each month on the road, neglecting their homes and gardens, if they had any. Once a year there was a distribution of cheap blankets and shoddy clothing. The self-respect of the people was almost fatally injured by these methods. This demoralizing ration-giving has been gradually done away with as the Indians progressed toward self-support, but is still found necessary in many cases.

Not all features of reservation life are bad; for while many good things are shut out and some evils flourish, others are excluded. Liquor traffic among Indians has been forbidden by law since the colonial period; and the law is fairly well enforced by a number of special officers; yet in a few tribes there has been in recent years much demoralization through liquor. It is generally admitted that there is less crime and rowdyism on the reservations than in civilized communities of equal size. In 1878 a force of native police was authorized to keep order, eject intruders, act as truant officers, and perform other duties under the direction of the agent. Though paid only ten or twelve dollars a month, these men have been faithful and efficient in the performance of duties involving considerable hardship and sometimes danger. Their loyalty and patriotism are deserving of special praise. In making arrests and bringing in desperate prisoners, as in the case of Pretty Elk the Brule Sioux murderer, and of the chief, Sitting Bull, the faithful police have sometimes lost their lives.

INDIAN CLAIMS

It is commonly admitted that the Indian treaties have been frequently broken by the United States, both in the letter and the spirit, while, on the other hand, the Indians have acted in good faith and with a high regard for their national honor. It is also a fact not very creditable to the Government that treaties have been materially amended in the Senate and not again submitted to the tribe, who were not even made aware at once of their altered provisions. I believe this would be considered a piece of sharp practice in the case of any people able to defend itself.

The breach of treaty obligations on the part of this Government has led to a large number of Indian claims, involving millions of dollars, which represent the efforts of tribes or bands which feel themselves wronged or defrauded to obtain justice under the white man's law. The history of one or two such may be of interest.

Most of the Oneida and Stockbridge tribes exchanged their New York reservations for a large tract of land in Kansas, and started for their new home in 1830, but never got any farther than Green Bay, Wisconsin. There the Menominees invited them to remain and share their reservation, as they had plenty of good land. The Stockbridges had originally occupied the beautiful Housatonic valley, where Jonathan Edwards preached to them and made them good Presbyterians; nevertheless, the "Christian" colonists robbed them of their homes and drove them westward. They did not resist the aggression. If anything is proved in history, it is that those who follow in the footsteps of the meek and gentle Jesus will be treated unmercifully, as he was, by a hard and material world.

These Stockbridges went still further with their kind hosts, and ultimately both tribes accepted the hospitality of the Ojibways. They made their unfortunate brothers welcome, and made them a free gift of land. But now observe the white man's sense of honor and justice in glaring contrast! For seventy-five years the United States Government failed to recompense these people for their Kansas land, which they never reached, and which in the meantime was taken up by settlers, and gradually covered with thriving homes and fertile farms.

The whole case was scrutinized again and again by the Congress of the United States from 1830 to about 1905, when at last a payment was made! The fact that the two tribes remained in Wisconsin and settled there does not invalidate their claim, as those wild Ojibways had no treaty with the Government at that time and had a perfect right to give away some of their land. It was a barefaced, open steal from the Indians. Yet the tribes were obliged to employ white attorneys at a liberal per cent. of the amount they hoped to recover. They had to pay high for simple justice. Meanwhile they lived on their own labor for two or three generations, and contributed to the upbuilding of Wisconsin. To-day some of them are doing better than their white neighbors.

This is only one illustration of a not uncommon happening; for, while some of these claims are doubtless unreasonable, I personally know of many in which the ethics of the case are as clear as in this which I have cited. It is often the fact that differences among attorneys and party politics in Congress delay justice for many years or deprive the Indians of their rights altogether. A bill has recently been introduced, at the instance of the Society of American Indians, which is framed to permit Indian tribes to sue in the Court of Claims, without first obtaining the consent of Congress in each case. This bill ought to be at once made law, as it would do away within a few years with many long-drawn-out disputes and much waste and worse than waste of time and money.

CHAPTER IV

THE NEW INDIAN POLICY

I have tried to state plainly some of the difficulties found so harassing in adjusting the relations of the native and white races in America. While there have been terrible and most un-Christian mistakes in dealing with the Indian (who has always been fully able to appreciate fair play and to resent the lack of it), it is equally true that there has been of late years a serious effort to bring him within the bounds of modern progress, so that he may eventually adapt himself to the general life of the nation. Until recently he himself preferred to remain just outside the borders of civilization, and was commonly assumed to be incapable of advance or change.

The birth of the new era really dates from Abraham Lincoln's refusal to order the execution of three hundred Sioux braves, whom a military court had, in less than two days, convicted of murder and condemned to be hung, in order to satisfy the clamor of the citizens of Minnesota. They demanded to be avenged for the loss of friends, relatives, and property in the outbreak of 1862, and they forgot that these Sioux had been defrauded of the finest country in the world, their home, their living, and even cheated out of the ten cents per acre agreed to be paid for millions of acres of the choicest land. They had shown their teeth at last, after more than a century of patience and self-control.

The great President personally reviewed the records of the court, and wrote with his own hand the names of the forty Indians who were executed, instead of three hundred originally condemned to die. He was abused and insulted for his humanity. Governor Ramsey of Minnesota appealed to him in vain in the name of the frontier people: that gentle, brave, just President had his way, and many of those whom he pardoned afterward became leaders of the Sioux in walking the white man's road.

INDIAN REFORMS UNDER GRANT

During General Grant's administration the famous "Peace Policy" made a remarkable start in the face of the determined resistance of the Plains Indians. The Indian, when making his last stand against injustice, is a desperate and a dangerous enemy. It was estimated at this time that every warrior killed in battle had cost the Government twenty-three lives and a round million of dollars. At this rate, the race would not be "wiped out" for generations. Kindness would be infinitely cheaper, as well as more pleasing, doubtless, to the white man's God!

In a word, Christian men and women came tardily to the conclusion that something more consistent with the claims of their religion must be shown these brave people who had lost everything in the face of the herculean advance of the dominant race. Reflection upon the sordid history of their country's dealings with the red man had taught them to think clearly, above the clamor of the self-seeking mob. Some of them had lived side by side with their dusky neighbors, and studied them at close range, in the light of broad human feeling. Such men were General Grant, Bishops Whipple and Hare, William Welsh and his nephew, Herbert Welsh of Philadelphia, Commissioner of Indian Affairs Smith, General Armstrong, and General Pratt. No class or sect has more fully endorsed this policy than have the Quakers, of whom the late Albert K. Smiley of Mohonk Conference fame was a distinguished representative.

In 1870 President Grant placed all Indian agencies under the control of the various churches and missionary organizations, which had hitherto been practically the sole channels of educational or uplift work among the tribes. Undoubtedly Grant sincerely wished to put an end to official corruption in this branch of the service, and to make the best possible use of all moneys that might be appropriated for Indian civilization, when he took the radical step of inviting each of the denominations interested to name the agent at one or more agencies, their candidate to hold office as long as he enjoyed their confidence, and to choose his own subordinates. It was confidently hoped that by this means the civil and religious work might be in full harmony, and that the Indians, instead of being hopelessly confused by conflicting views and practices among their would-be teachers, might learn equally by precept and example.

Grant's policy remained in force for about ten years, and there is no question that in this short space of time the churches accomplished wonders among the raw Sioux but lately confined to their reservations. The following agencies of which I had personal knowledge were then industrious Christian communities: namely, Sisseton under the Presbyterians, Devil's Lake under the Catholics, Yankton under the Episcopalians, Santee under the Quakers. Winnebagoes, Pawnees, Omahas, all the wild Plains Indians did well under consistent and conscientious management. Large fields of wheat were cultivated by them, with but little assistance, which have since gone back to wild land under the "spoils system," and over which, ten years ago, I hunted prairie chickens.

There were developed during this period many strong Christians of a genuinely apostolic stamp, who became teachers and preachers to their wilder brethren. Both children and adults were taught to read in their own language, and at least two papers were published monthly in the Sioux tongue, which had been reduced to writing by the Riggses and Williamsons, the earliest Protestant missionaries. It was then and there that I myself received my impetus toward an education. My father, who was one of the two hundred and sixty Sioux pardoned by Lincoln, had voluntarily abandoned the reservation with its pauperizing influences, and was a self-supporting citizen in 1870.

Another interesting feature of Grant's administration was the number of Indians holding responsible positions in the service. At a time when there were no great Indian schools, there were found and trained men competent to act as agency blacksmiths, carpenters, millers, etc. There was even a full-blood Iroquois at the head of the Indian Bureau--Grant's chief of staff, General Ely Parker.

THE WARS OF THE SECTS

It was a genuine calamity for our people when this system was overthrown, as it was in a few years, by the clamor of the politicians for patronage, together with the sectarian disputes that have been a scandal to the heathen throughout the history of Christian missions. On many reservations proselyting work had been begun by two or more denominations, and these bodies now became rivals, even bitter and hostile rivals, for the souls and bodies of their reputed converts. To the Catholics, in particular, who claimed thirty-eight of the seventy-two agencies, on the ground of prior religious influence, there had been assigned but eight. Strong pressure was brought to bear through their Bureau of Missions to reverse this ruling; and equally strong, or stronger, was the political pressure for the rich spoils of the Indian agencies. By 1883 Grant's too idealistic system broke down entirely, the fat offices were returned to the politicians, and all denominations were permitted to engage at will in missionary propaganda, but without secular authority.

A certain chief in the Red River region well expressed a view common among our people when he said to the priest: "You tell us that we can be saved only if we accept your faith and are baptized by you. The Protestant minister tells us the same. Yet both claim to worship the same God! Who shall judge between you? We have considered the matter, and decided that when your two roads join we will follow you; but until then we prefer our own religion!"

Nevertheless it was largely through the influence of the missionaries and their converts that in most of the treaties made during this period there were inserted clauses providing for the practical education of the Indian children. There has been much fraud connected with the purchase of materials and supplies, and in every way that shrewd and unprincipled men can devise, but even the politicians could not entirely prevent the building of those schools. One fact stands out boldly: it was the Christian missionary, in spite of serious mistakes, who played the most important part in the transformation of the Indian and the development of the West.

MODERN "FRIENDS OF THE INDIAN"

From this time on the old view of the Indian as a hopeless savage has been gradually abandoned, and replaced by the juster modern view which regards him as essentially a man, and as good material for the future citizen. The volunteer organizations arising under Grant and continuing active to the present day have been effective molders of public opinion along these lines.

The Boston Indian Citizenship Committee was organized in 1879, on the occasion of the forcible removal of the Poncas to Indian Territory. Chief Standing Bear and the Indian maiden Bright Eyes (Susette La Flesche) visited many leading cities and told eloquently the story of their wrongs. They were ultimately restored to their old home, largely through the efforts of this group of influential men. The committee then undertook to secure citizenship for Indians on the basis of taxation, a principle that was denied by the Supreme Court; but a few years later the same end was attained by the passage of the "Dawes bill." Since then they have endeavored to secure honest allotments to Indians, to prevent the sale of the best lands to whites at nominal prices, and to obtain the dismissal of corrupt Indian agents and inspectors.

The National Indian Association, composed chiefly of women, began work with a memorial to Congress in 1879, and has continued it until now, under the efficient leadership of Mrs. A. S. Quinton, Mrs. Sara T. Kinney, and others. The missionary department has established fifty pioneer missions in as many neglected tribes or tribal remnants, turning them over ultimately, with their buildings and plant, to the mission boards of the various Protestant denominations. The society has also fostered native industries, being the mother of the Indian Industries League; has loaned money to Indians for home-building; assisted in the education of especially promising individuals; built and supported hospitals, and done other valuable work. Its headquarters are in New York City.

The Indian Rights Association was organized in Philadelphia, in 1882, at the home of Mr. John Welsh. Mr. Herbert Welsh has been for many years its leading spirit, and others who have done yeoman's service in the cause are the late Professor Painter, Mr. Brosius, and Mr. Matthew K. Sniffen. Its slogan was the same as that of the others: Education; Land in Severalty; Citizenship! To all three of these bodies, as well as to the Board of Indian Commissioners, belongs much credit for urging the reforms which triumphed, in 1887, in the "Dawes bill," the Emancipation Act of the Indian.

The Indian Rights Association maintains a representative in Washington to cooperate with the Indian Bureau and to keep an eye upon legislation affecting the tribes, as well as a permanent office in Philadelphia. Its officers and agents have kept in close touch with developments in the field, and have conducted many investigations on Indian agencies, resulting often in the exposure of grave abuses. They have been courageous and aggressive in their work, and have not hesitated to appeal to the courts when necessary to protect the rights of Indians. They have also done much to mold public sentiment through meetings, letters to the press, and the circulation of their own literature to the number of more than half a million copies.

One of President Grant's first acts was the creation, in 1869, of the United States Board of Indian Commissioners, a body of ten men supposed to be "eminent for their intelligence and philanthropy," to serve without pay in an advisory capacity, and to cooperate with the Interior Department in securing a sound and progressive administration of Indian affairs. The only appropriation is for travelling expenses and for a salaried secretary with an office in Washington. It has been one of the important duties of this Board to inspect the Indian supplies when purchased, if possible securing goods up to the standard of the samples submitted and preventing open fraud. Its members have travelled extensively in the Indian country in order to observe conditions, and their patriotic services have been appreciated by both races.

In the autumn of 1883 Mr. Albert K. Smiley, the large-hearted owner of a hostelry overlooking beautiful Lake Mohonk, in the Shawangum range, invited a number of prominent Indian workers to meet as his guests for discussion of actual conditions and necessary reforms. With this historic meeting began an uninterrupted series of "Mohonk Indian Conferences," at which missionaries of all denominations, Government officials, members of Congress, representatives of philanthropic societies, teachers in Indian schools, editors, ministers, and other influential men and women, with a sprinkling of educated Indians, meet annually at the call of Mr. Smiley, and since his death in 1912 at that of his brother, Mr. Daniel Smiley, to discuss all matters bearing upon the welfare of the race in a sympathetic atmosphere and amid the pleasantest surroundings. Mr. Smiley was a member of the Board of Indian Commissioners, and for many years these conferences were closely connected with the affairs of the Board, and the proceedings were published as a part of its annual report.

The platform adopted each year at Lake Mohonk is widely circulated, and has had much influence; although, as it represents only the unanimous vote of a body among whom there actually exist wide differences of opinion, it is not always as satisfactory as it might be. It has seemed to some who attended the early conferences that those of late years have been less fruitful, owing partly to less novelty in the subject-matter and to the sharing of the time with problems of Hawaii and the Philippines, and partly to a desire for unanimity and good feeling that has kept unpleasant facts from the light. It is certain that the debates are more carefully pre-arranged and therefore less spontaneous.

The Mohonk Conferences have consistently recommended larger appropriations for Indian education; the extension of the laws of the land over Indian reservations; the gradual withdrawal of rations; the allotment of communal land to individuals, and more recently the breaking up of the tribal trust funds into individual holdings. Emphasis has been laid upon the need of greater care in selecting men of character as Indian agents and superintendents. The thirty-first conference urges a vigorous campaign against tuberculosis, trachoma, and other diseases among Indians, also against the liquor traffic, and mescal habit, and declares that the proposition to control Indian affairs through a non-partisan commission to serve during long terms is "worthy of serious consideration." It also makes special recommendations in behalf of the Pueblo, the Navajo, the Five Civilized Tribes of Oklahoma, and the New York Indians, looking toward their present protection and future citizenship.

These "Eastern sentimentalists," as they have often been called by persons interested in depriving the red man of his heritage, have pursued their ends steadily, though not without severe setbacks. The opposition to Indian schools in Congress was for many years very strong, but it has now almost ceased, except in sporadic instances. One seldom hears it said nowadays that "the only good Indian is the dead Indian," and the Western Senator who declared that "you could no more civilize an Apache than you could civilize a rattlesnake" would rather shock than convince his hearers in the light of present-day progress. The greatest enemy to Indian civilization has been the return of the "spoils system" in the eighties, and the formation of a corrupt "Indian ring" whose ramifications extended so deep and so high that even the most sincere and disinterested despaired of obtaining justice. Yet the average American citizen honestly wants to give the Indian a fair chance!

To sum up, he had been an indomitable foe, and occupied a vast region which by 1870 was already beat upon by the tides of settlement. Two things were determined upon: First, he must be induced, bribed, or forced to enter the reservation. Second, he must be trained and persuaded to adopt civilized life, and so saved to the future if he proved to be worth saving, which many doubted. In order to carry out these projects his wild food supply had to be ruthlessly cut off, and the buffalo were of necessity sacrificed.

Here is a system which has gradually taken its present complicated form during two thousand years. A primitive race has put it on ready made, to a large extent, within two generations. In order to accomplish such a feat, they had to fight physical demoralization, psychological confusion, and spiritual apathy. In other words, the old building had to be pulled down, foundations and all, and replaced by the new. But you have had to use the same timber!

CHAPTER V

THE INDIAN IN SCHOOL

The thought of educating the natives of America was first conceived by the earliest explorer-priests, prompted by ecclesiastical ambition and religious zeal. Churches and missionary societies among the early colonists undertook both to preach and teach among the children of the forest, who, said they, "must either be moralized or exterminated." Schools and missions were established and maintained among them by the mother churches in England and Scotland, and in a few cases by the colonists themselves. It was provided in the charters of our oldest colleges that a certain number of Indian pupils should be educated therein, and others, as Dartmouth and Hamilton, were founded primarily for Indian youth. The results, though meagre, were on the whole deserving of consideration. In the middle of the eighteenth century there were said to be some Indian boys in Stockbridge, Mass., who "read English well," and at Harvard several excelled in the classics. Joseph Brant, though a terror to the colonists during the Revolution, was a man of rare abilities and considerable education; and Samson Occum, the most famous educated Indian of his day, was not only an eloquent preacher and successful teacher but an accomplished hymn-writer. The visit of "the great Mohegan" to England in 1765, when he preached more than three hundred times and raised some ten thousand pounds for Dartmouth College, was perhaps the most striking incident of his career.

From this early chapter of Indian education we find it clearly proven that individual red men were able to assimilate the classical culture of the period, and capable, moreover, of loyalty toward the new ideals no less than the old. The utter disregard of hygiene then prevalent, and the further facts that industrial training was neglected and little or no attention paid to the girls, would account to the modern mind for many disappointments. However, most of the so-called "failure" of this work is directly traceable to unjust laws, social segregation, frequent wars, strong drink, and the greed of the whites for Indian lands, one or all of which causes destroyed many promising beginnings and exterminated whole tribes or drove them from well-established homes into poverty and exile.

EARLY MISSION AND CONTRACT SCHOOLS

Beginning with the first years of the nineteenth century, practically every religious denomination in America carried on more or less educational work among the natives. In some cases the Indians themselves contributed toward the expense of these schools, and in others the United States Government gave meagre aid. As early as 1775 the Continental Congress had appropriated five hundred dollars for the support and education of youths at Dartmouth College. This was, however, less an act of benevolence than of self-interest, since its avowed object was to conciliate the friendship of those Indians who might be inclined to ally themselves with the British during the struggle for independence.

From the year 1819 to 1848 ten thousand dollars annually was distributed by the Government among mission schools of various denominations, and in the latter year there were one hundred and three such schools, with over three thousand pupils. In 1870 the appropriation was increased to one hundred thousand; and about 1873, during Grant's administration, already described as marking a new era for the red man, the Government began to develop a school system of its own, but did not therefore discontinue its aid to the mission boards. On the contrary, such aid was largely increased in the form of "contracts."

The usual rule was to pay a fixed sum (commonly $167 per capita per annum) for each pupil actually in attendance, the religious society or individual to whom the contract was given providing buildings, teachers, and equipment. It does not appear that there was any unjust discrimination between religious bodies in the application of these funds, and the fact that in the course of a few years a large and increasing proportion passed under the control of the Bureau of Catholic Indian Missions must be attributed entirely to their superior enterprise and activity. This was a period of awakening and rapid growth. By 1886 the total appropriations for Indian education had risen to more than $1,000,000, and the contracts aggregated $31,000. In ten years more the Catholics alone drew $314,000. But, during this decade, the policy of assisting sectarian schools with the public money, claimed to be a violation of the American principle of separation of Church and State, had been continuously under fire; and in 1895 it was finally decided by Congress to reduce the contracts 20 per cent. each year until abolished.

Meantime, the Methodists first in 1892, followed by all the other Protestant bodies, voluntarily relinquished their contracts, but the Catholics kept up the fight to the end; nevertheless, in 1900, all Congressional appropriations for sectarian schools were finally withdrawn.

Naturally this reversal of a policy of such long standing, even though due notice had been given, worked serious hardship to schools established in the expectation of its continuance. Bishop Hare's valuable work in South Dakota was crippled, particularly as the principle at issue was so interpreted by the Indian office as to forbid the issue of treaty rations to children enrolled in mission schools, although they would have received such rations had they not been in school at all.

It was held by the Bureau of Catholic Indian missions that Indian treaty and trust funds are in a different class from moneys derived from the taxpayers, and that it is perfectly legitimate for a tribe to assign a portion of its own revenues to the support of a mission school. The Supreme Court has since declared this view to be correct, and accordingly this church still utilizes tribal funds to a considerable amount each year. Rations were also restored to certain schools by act of Congress in 1906.

As in the case of the sectarian protests against President Grant's policy in regard to manning the Indian agencies, I believe that religious prejudice has been a real misfortune to our people. General Armstrong, in an address given at Lake Mohonk in 1890, expressed the well-founded opinion that the industrial work of the Catholic schools is as good as any, often superior; the academic work generally inferior, while on the moral and religious side he found them at their best.

CARLISLE AND HAMPTON

The Carlisle School in Pennsylvania was the first non-reservation boarding school to be established, a pioneer and a leader in this important class of schools, of which there are now thirty-five, scattered throughout the Middle and Western States. General R. H. Pratt (then Lieutenant Pratt), while in charge of Indian prisoners of war at Saint Augustine, Florida, made important reforms in their treatment, which led in 1878, when their release was ordered by the War Department, to a request on the part of twenty-two of the younger men for further education. Seventeen of these were received at Hampton Institute, Virginia, General Armstrong's celebrated school for freedmen, and the next year an Indian department was organized at Hampton, while General Pratt was authorized, at his own suggestion, to establish an Indian school in the abandoned army barracks at Carlisle.

The school opened with 147 pupils. There were many difficulties and much unintelligent opposition in the beginning, but wonderful success attended General Pratt's administration. For many years Carlisle has enrolled about 1,200 pupils each year, keeping almost half of them on farms and in good homes in Pennsylvania and New Jersey, where they work for board and wages in summer, while a smaller number attend the public school during the colder months. They earn and save about thirty thousand dollars annually. This "outing system" was devised by General Pratt, and has been adopted elsewhere, though not always with equal success.

Periodical attacks have been made upon the Carlisle school, usually from political or purely selfish motives; but it has survived them all. General Pratt's policy was to take the young Indian wholly out of his environment and the motives as well as the habits of his former life, and in support of it he has opposed some of the methods of the missionaries. His advice to his graduates is to remain east and compete in civilization. He has worked with tremendous energy and great single-mindedness, and has often been undiplomatic in his criticisms, thus incurring some enmity. But, upon the whole, his theory is the very backbone of Indian education, and in fact we are following it to-day.

It is the impression of the most advanced members of the race that he has rendered to them and to the country a particular service, and that the wonderful progress demonstrated by the Indian in recent years is due in large measure to his work, and to its results as seen at Hampton and Carlisle. These schools are visited by hundreds of people every year, and have furnished a convincing object-lesson to the many who opposed Indian education on theory alone. The other thirty-four non-reservation schools were secured with comparative ease after he had proved his case.

The Indian department at Hampton Institute, which opened in 1878 with General Pratt's seventeen prisoners of war, flourished for more than thirty years, and provided for the education of more than one hundred Indian pupils each year in "the hand, the heart, and the head." General Armstrong, one of America's heroes of peace, was an enthusiastic champion of the red man's cause, and as an object-lesson to the public, as well as in training native teachers and leaders, his great school has contributed much to the new era. It was decided by Congress a year or two ago to withdraw the Government appropriation of $20,000 annually from the Hampton school, but notwithstanding this, more than thirty Indian pupils remain to work their way through, with some assistance from free scholarships.

Hampton claims to have been the first school to begin keeping systematic records of its returned Indian students, and by means of these records the school is able to show satisfactory and encouraging results of its work for

Indians.

In reply to the oft-asked question: "Do educated Indians go back to the blanket?" it should be said, first, that return to Indian dress in isolated communities where this is still the common dress of the people is not necessarily retrogression. It may be only a wise conformity to custom. Investigation has shown, however, that very few graduates of any school ever do reassume Indian dress or ways. Of those who have attended school but two or three years in all, a larger proportion may do so. A northwestern school reports that out of a total of 234 graduates only three are known to be failures. The most recent Carlisle report shows that of 565 living graduates, all but 69 are known to be profitably employed in a wide variety of occupations; 110 are in the Government service. There are also 3,800 ex-students, not graduates, of whom a large majority are successful. Hampton has 878 living returned Indian students, of whom 87 per cent. are recorded as doing well.

In 1897 the Indian Bureau required all Indian agents and superintendents to report upon the conduct and usefulness of every student returned from a non-reservation school. Such an investigation was sure not to be unduly favorable, and the report showed 76 per cent. of successes. In 1901 a more careful inquiry raised it to 86 per cent.

MISSION SCHOOLS OF TO-DAY

It must not be supposed that the downfall of the contract system and the development of Government work has meant the end of distinctively mission schools for Indians. Although a few have been closed, there are still many in successful operation under the various church boards, the Indians themselves willingly contributing to their support. Indeed, this feature of partial self-support is much in their favor, as it is certain that an education that costs the recipient something is of more worth.

Except for a few plants taken over by the Government, the Catholics continue to conduct their fine agricultural boarding-schools, notably those among the Sioux. Bishop Hare of the Episcopal Church began his labors among the same people in 1873; and in nothing was his statesmanlike breadth of mind more clearly shown than in the foundation of a system of excellent boarding-schools, of which at one time there were five under his watchful care, where from thirty to seventy children each were sheltered and taught in the atmosphere of a sunny Christian home. It was impossible to carry them all after the discontinuance of all Government aid, either in money or rations, but, although the Bishop died in 1909, Saint Mary's at Rosebud and Saint Elizabeth's at Standing Rock remain a monument to his memory.

The Presbyterian Church conducts two successful boarding and a number of day schools; and the Congregationalists have concentrated their efforts upon a large training-school at Santee, Nebraska, under the veteran missionary teacher, Rev. Alfred L. Riggs. At Santee the Indian boys and girls are given a practical education developed to fit their peculiar needs--its goal the training of teachers, preachers, and leaders in every walk of life. Here I received my first impulse toward a career in 1875-6. In all these schools, even those where the material equipment is insufficient, there is more emphasis upon character-building, more of permanence and in general higher qualifications in the teaching force than under Government.

VIRTUES AND DEFECTS OF THE PRESENT SYSTEM

There has been nearly $90,000,000 appropriated by Congress since 1876 for Indian education. The appropriation for 1915 was over $4,500,000. Yet even more is needed. The Indian Bureau estimates 77,000 Indian children of school age; of these about 27,000 are provided for in Government schools, 4,000 in mission and 25,000 in public schools, leaving about 20,000 entirely neglected, besides an estimated 7,000 sick and defective children, who need hospital schools or some form of special care.

The present system includes day and boarding schools on the reservations, as well as the large industrial schools off the reservations. In 1913 there were reported two hundred and twenty-three day schools and seventy-six reservation boarding-schools. The training in the former is elementary; and the most advanced goes little beyond the eighth grammar grade in the public school, though at Carlisle and a few others there are short normal and business courses. In 1882 a superintendent was appointed to inspect and correlate these widely scattered institutions, and a few years later a corps of supervisors was put in the field. Since 1891 there have been institutes and summer schools conducted for the benefit of the teachers.

It is the rule in all boarding-schools that one half the time of each pupil be given to industrial work, which includes most of the labor involved in running the kitchen, dining-room, laundry, sewing-room, and school farm or garden, as well as systematic training in housekeeping, agriculture, and the mechanical trades. The age of graduation is usually from seventeen to twenty-five or even more. This retardation is to be attributed partly to the half-day system; partly to frequent transfers from one school to another, and consequent loss of grade; and in the poorer schools to inefficiency of teachers and lack of ambition on the part of pupils. It must be remembered, moreover, that the subjects and methods of study, in language, mathematics, and abstract ideas of all kinds, were entirely foreign to the untutored Indian mind. It is difficult to study in a foreign language even when the subject of study is familiar; the Indian student is expected to master subjects absolutely unknown to him in his own life. Yet I have heard teachers experienced in public school work declare that these children of nature are as responsive as white children; in writing and drawing they excel; and discipline is easier, at least among the wilder tribes. The result in thirty or forty years has opened the eyes of many who heretofore held the theory that the Indian will always remain Indian.

Admitting that these schools compare well with state institutions which are on a similar basis, and are controlled by political appointments, there are some abuses, as might be expected. While there are fine men in charge of certain schools, there are others who are neither efficient nor sympathetic with the cause of Indian uplift. Most regrettable is the fact that the moral influence of such schools has been at different times very low. The pupils themselves have come to look upon them as political institutions and to discard all genuine effort. It is a case of serve the master and he will not bother you; all else is merely show. I believe that there has been some improvement in recent years, chiefly on account of the protection given by the rules of the civil service. Let the teacher set an example of honest living and the scholar will be sure to follow; but if the one is a hypocrite, the other will become one. Remember, you have induced or forced the Indian mother to give up her five and six year old children on your promise to civilize, educate, Christianize--but not subsidize or commercialize them!

Some of the reservations are oversupplied with schools, while others, notably the Navajo, have almost none. In the former case, the Indian parents are kept in an anxious state and often very unhappy. Since the Indian Bureau has required the superintendent to keep up his quota of pupils, or the number of teachers and the total appropriation will be reduced in proportion, he may be compelled, as some one has said, to "rob the cradle and the grave"--in other words, he is not careful to omit those under age and the sickly ones. Much harm has been done by placing children in an advanced stage of tuberculosis in the same dormitory with healthy youngsters. Irregular attendance is too often tolerated; and a serious evil is the admission of children of well-to-do parents, who dress their young folks extravagantly, supply them with unlimited spending money, and who, in all reason, should be required to pay for their support and education.

Another drawback lies in the fact that each new Commissioner of Indian Affairs, usually a man without special knowledge or experience in the complex work over which he is called to preside, comes out with a scheme for reforming the whole system. Perhaps he advocates doing away with Carlisle and the schools of its class, and places all the emphasis upon the little day schools in the Indian camps; or it may be vice versa. All the advance we have made is through all of these schools; we cannot spare any of them. We should be a thousand times better off if the reformers could rid us of the professional politicians, but I fear this is impossible. I have abandoned all hope of it, after long experience both in the field and in Washington. I would give up anything rather than the schools, unmoral as many of them are. The pupils become every year better fitted to choose and to combat the evil in their environment. They will soon be able to prepare themselves for the new life without taking notice of what does not concern them. I rejoice in every real gain; and I predict that the Indian will soon adjust himself fully to the requirements of the age, be able to appreciate its magnificent achievements, and contribute his mite to the modern development of the land of his ancestors.

CHAPTER VI

THE INDIAN AT HOME

Although among the graduates and ex-students of the Indian schools there are now some in almost every modern occupation, including commerce, the trades and professions, the great majority of these young people, as of their fellow tribesmen who lack an English education, are farmers, ranchers, and stockmen. Nearly all Indians own some land, either individually or in common; and while it may generally be leased by those who are either unable or for good reasons do not desire to work it themselves, this is done under such troublesome restrictions and conditions that it is, as a general rule, better for the owner to live on and utilize his allotment. Of course this is a rule that admits of many exceptions.

THE PROBLEM OF SELF-SUPPORT

Since most Indian reservations are in the arid belt and the greater portion of the land is therefore unsuited to agriculture, at least without extensive irrigation, perhaps the larger number of the men are stock-raisers, an occupation well suited to the Plains Indians, who are great riders and very fond of their horses. They raise both horses and cattle, and many have become well-to-do from this source. From time to time their herds are improved by well-bred stallions and mares and blooded cattle, furnished by the Government under treaty stipulations. The total valuation of stock belonging to Indians, both individual and tribal, is now twenty-two million dollars in round numbers, according to the tables furnished by the Indian Bureau. This estimate includes sheep, goats, and poultry. The Navajoes, who number about 22,000 and are in a fairly primitive state, having few schools or missionaries among them, are thrifty and successful sheep-herders and entirely self-supporting. The value of crops raised by Indians during the last fiscal year is estimated at more than four millions.

In a word, the typical red man of to-day is a rancher on a large or small scale. He has displayed quite as much intelligence and aptitude for the work as could be expected. There have been serious handicaps, other than the tradition among us that the cultivation of the soil is a feminine rather than a manly occupation. I may mention the occupation of the best lands by white settlers, with or without our consent; the ration system; and the "spoils system" as applied to the appointment of our superintendents and instructors in farming.

Take the Sioux, for example--a strong and self-respecting people who had shown a willingness to fight for their rights when it became necessary. They were presently corralled upon reservations in a land of little rain, and given enough food to sustain life, under a solemn engagement to continue feeding "until they became self-supporting." There was scant opportunity and still less inducement to become so; accordingly only a few of the more ambitious or energetic worked at teaming or whatever they could get to do, improved their homes, acquired stock, and gradually fought their way upward. For many years this clause in the treaty was not applied to individuals; that is, it was interpreted to mean that all should receive rations until all became self-supporting. Twenty years ago, when I lived among them as agency doctor, Government and mission workers of Indian blood, well-to-do mixed bloods, and intermarried white men all drew their rations regularly, with very few exceptions.

About a dozen years ago tardy steps were taken to carry out the evident intention of the treaty, which had hitherto been defeated by keeping it to the letter. Rations were withdrawn from all who had other sufficient means of support. This seemed like imposing a penalty upon industry; but it was soon followed by requiring all able-bodied men to perform a certain amount of labor for the common benefit, such as road-making, bridge building, etc., in return for money or rations. This was a great advance even though accompanied by some evils, notably the neglect of allotments while their families camped with the gangs of laborers on different parts of the reservation. Later, the same credit was allowed for days' labor performed in improving their own homesteads and putting up hay for their cattle. More cows and better farming implements have been issued in recent years, and there is a wholesome effort to make the work of the so-called agency or "district farmers" less of a farce than it has often been in the past.

These farmers number about 250 and are employees of the Indian service. They are supposed to instruct and assist the Indians of their respective districts in modern methods of agriculture; but there has been a time, probably not altogether past, when they were occupied chiefly in drawing water, filling ice-houses, and a variety of similar "chores" for the agent and his subordinates. In many cases they themselves knew little of practical farming, or their experience lay in a soil and climate utterly unlike that of the Indian country to which they came.

Hon. Cato Sells, the present Commissioner of Indian Affairs, states in his first annual report that he is placing more emphasis upon agriculture than upon any other activity of the Indian Bureau. He requires the farmers to make their homes in the districts to which they are assigned, and to keep in close touch with the people. They are furnished with modern agricultural text-books, and demonstration farms or experiment stations are maintained at convenient points. Thirty-seven practical stockmen have also been employed to give special attention to this part of the work, and the Indians are said to be cooperating intelligently in the effort to improve their breeding stock.

At certain agencies farming implements and seed are loaned to Indians who have no other means of securing them, and hundreds who have been so helped are meeting their payments when due with commendable promptness. Agricultural fairs have been held in recent years at twenty or more Indian agencies, arousing much local interest, and an increasing number of Indian farmers are taking part in county and state fairs.

In several of the Northwestern States the value of the timber on Indian lands is enormous; the latest official estimate is eighty-four million dollars. If the Indian had been allowed to cut his own pine and run his own sawmills, we should now have native lumber kings as well as white. This is not permitted, however; and a paternal Government sells the stumpage for the benefit of its wards, who are fortunate if the money received for it has not seeped out of the official envelope or withered away of the prevailing disease called "political consumption."

The irrigation force of the Bureau consists of an inspector and seven subordinates, who supervise irrigation projects on the various reservations, upon which more than half a million dollars was expended during the last fiscal year. The protection of water rights, notably those of the Pimas in Arizona, a peaceful and industrious tribe who have suffered severely from the loss of their water at the hands of unprincipled white men, is of primary importance.

Oil and gas, especially in Oklahoma, are proving enormously valuable, and are being mined under leases executed by the Bureau. Many Indians are becoming well-to-do from the payment of royalties, but it cannot be doubted that the biggest prizes go, as usual, to our white brothers.

The Indian office maintains an employment bureau to assist in finding profitable work for Indians, particularly returned students, and I am informed from trustworthy sources that it has met with fair success. It is headed by a Carlisle graduate, Charles E. Dagenett, who was trained for a business career. Considerable numbers of Indians, particularly in the Southwest, are provided with employment in the sugar-beet fields, in harvesting canteloupes and other fruits, in railroad construction, irrigation projects, and other fields of activity, and it appears that their work gives general satisfaction.

INDIAN WOMEN AS HOME-MAKERS

Probably the average white man still believes that the Indian woman of the old days was little more than a beast of burden to her husband. But the missionary who has lived among his people, the sympathetic observer of their every-day life, holds a very different opinion. You may generally see the mother and her babe folded close in one shawl, indicating the real and most important business of her existence. Without the child, life is but a hollow play, and all Indians pity the couple who are unable to obey the primary command, the first law of real happiness.

She has always been the silent but telling power behind life's activities, and at the same time shared equally with her mate the arduous duties of primitive society. Possessed of true feminine dignity and modesty, she was expected to be his equal in physical endurance and skill, but his superior in spiritual insight. She was looked to for the endowment of her child with nature's gifts and powers, and no woman of any race has ever come closer to universal mother-hood.

She was the spiritual teacher of the child, as well as its tender nurse, and she brought its developing soul before the "Great Mystery" as soon as she was aware of its coming. When she had finished her work, at the age of five to eight years, she turned her boy over to his father for manly training, and to the grandparents for traditional instruction, but the girl child remained under her close and thoughtful supervision. She preserved man from soul-killing materialism by herself owning what few possessions they had, and thus branding possession as feminine. The movable home was hers, with all its belongings, and she ruled there unquestioned. She was, in fact, the moral salvation of the race; all virtue was entrusted to her, and her position was recognized by all. It was held in all gentleness and discretion, under the rule that no woman could talk much or loudly until she became a grandmother.

The Indian woman suffered greatly during the transition period of civilization, when men were demoralized by whiskey, and possession became masculine. The division of labor did not readily adjust itself to the change, so that her burdens were multiplied while her influence decreased. Tribe after tribe underwent the catastrophe of a disorganized and disunited family life.

To-day, I am glad to say, we have still reason to thank our Indian mothers for the best part of our manhood. A great many of them are earnest Christian women, who have carried their native uprightness and devoted industry over into the new life. The annual reports of the missionaries show large sums, running into the thousands of dollars, raised by the self-denying labor of the native women for the support of their churches and other Christian work.

As the men have gradually assumed the responsibility of the outdoor toil, cultivating the fields and building the houses, the women have undertaken the complicated housekeeping tasks of their white sisters. It is true that until they understood the civilized way of cooking and the sanitation of stationary homes, the race declined in health and vigor. For the great improvement noticeable in these directions, much credit is due to the field matrons of the Indian Service.

The field matron is sometimes called the "Going-around woman," or the "Clean-up woman," and her house-to-house teaching and inspection is undoubtedly of much practical value. She is often the physician's right hand in follow-up work among his patients, especially the women and children. Some of the most efficient women in the service are themselves of Indian blood, such as Mrs. Annie Dawson Wilde of Fort Berthold, a graduate of Hampton and of a state normal school, who has given many years to this work. Similar instruction is sometimes given by day-school teachers and woman missionaries.

MARRIAGE AND THE FAMILY

The social morality of the various tribes differs very much at the present time. Under our original customs, the purity of woman and the home was safeguarded by strict rules, with severe penalties for their transgression. When, however, native customs were broken down without the efficient substitution of civilized laws, there was much social irregularity.

Plural marriages were permissible under our system, but were not very general, and plural wives were usually sisters. The missionaries, and in some instances the Federal authorities, have required elderly men to abandon all but one wife, leading to difficult problems. Many of the younger generation are now legally married, and an effort is made to oblige them to secure legal divorces when a separation is sought, but as some state courts hold that they have no jurisdiction to hear applications of non-citizen Indians living on reservations, this is often impracticable, and naturally the dissatisfied simply abandon wife or husband, and perhaps take another by Indian custom only. It is advisable that family records be more strictly kept than is now the case.

UNEDUCATED LEADERS AMONG INDIANS

I wish to refute the common misconception that it is only the educated and Christian Indian who has contributed to the progress of his people and to the common good of both races. There are many men wholly unlettered, and some of whom have not proclaimed themselves followers of Christ, who have yet exerted great influence on the side of civilization. Almost every tribe has a hero of this type who arose at a critical juncture to lead his fellows.

In the early part of the nineteenth century there was Little Turtle, a celebrated Miami chief, who, to be sure, defended his country bravely, but when he made a treaty he stood by it faithfully, and advocated peace and civilization for his people. The Pottawatomie chief Pokagon was another, whose son Simon Pokagon was prominent at the World's Fair in Chicago. A leading contemporary of these men was Keokuk of the Sacs and Foxes. Wabashaw the third, of the Mississippi Sioux, was known as a strong friend to civilization; and so was my own great-grandfather, Chief Cloud Man, whose village occupied the present site of the city of Minneapolis. His son, Appearing Sacred Stone, whose English name was David Weston, was a fine character--a hereditary chief who took a homestead at Flandreau and became a native preacher under Bishop Hare.

Chief Strike-the-Ree, by whose influence and diplomacy the Yankton Sioux were kept neutral throughout the Sioux wars; Lone Wolf of the Kiowas, Quanah Parker of the Comanches, whose mother was a white captive, and Governor James Big Heart of the Osages were all men of this type, natural leaders and statesmen. Iron Eyes, or Joseph La Flesche, a head chief of the Omahas, was a notable leader in progressive ways; and so is John Grass of the Blackfoot Sioux, also a distinguished orator.

Men like this, of native force and fire, but without advantages other than those shared by the mass of their people, are possibly more deserving of honor than are the few who have made the most of exceptional opportunities. If anything, they illustrate more clearly the innate capacity and moral strength of the race.

When it is considered that of the three hundred and odd thousand Indians in the United States, only about two thirds are still living on reservations under the control of the Indian Bureau, the official figures concerning that two thirds are surprising to most of us. We are told that 50,000 able-bodied adults are entirely self-supporting, and that only 17,000 Indians of all classes are receiving rations. Twenty-two thousand are employed on wages and salaries, earning more than two million dollars yearly. Three fourths of the families live in permanent houses; 100,000 persons speak English, and 161,000 wear citizen's clothing. Such is the average present-day Indian at home--a man who earns his own living, speaks the language of the country, wears its dress, and obeys its laws. Surely it is but one step further to American citizenship!

CHAPTER VII

THE INDIAN AS A CITIZEN

We have taken note of the reluctance of the American Indian to develop an organized community life, though few appreciate his reasons for preferring a simpler social ideal. As a matter of fact as well as sentiment, he was well content with his own customs and philosophy. Nevertheless, after due protest and resistance, he has accepted the situation; and, having accepted it, he is found to be easily governed by civilized law and usages. It has been demonstrated more than once that he is capable of sustaining a high moral and social standard when placed under wise guidance and at the same time protected from the barbarians of civilization.

MODEL INDIAN COMMUNITIES

William Duncan, an Englishman, came among a band of Alaskan natives about the middle of the last century, and they formed a strong mutual attachment. The friendship of these simple people was not misplaced, and Mr. Duncan did not misuse it for his own advantage, as is too apt to be the case with a white man. He adapted himself to their temperament and sense of natural justice, but gradually led them to prefer civilized habits and industries, and finally to accept the character of Christ as their standard. He used the forms of the Church of England, but modified them as good sense dictated.

They worked together in good faith for a generation; and as a result there was founded the Christian community of Metlakatla, Alaska, almost an ideal little republic, so long as no self-seeking Anglo-Saxon interfered with its workings. The Indians became carpenters, blacksmiths, farmers, gardeners, as well as better fishermen. They established a sawmill and a salmon cannery. They built houses and boats, and finally a steamboat, which was run by one of their number. Mr. Duncan never allowed strong drink to enter the colony; he was the only white man among a thousand Indians, and so strong was their faith in him that he was accepted as their leader both practically and spiritually. He devoted his whole life to them, and never married. Some of the young people he sent away to the States to school: among them Edward Marsden, a many-sided man, who is not only a graduate of a small college in Ohio and of a theological seminary, but has some knowledge of law and medicine, is an able seaman, and an efficient machinist.

The Metlakatlans are not technically citizens, though discharging many civic duties. In 1887 they were compelled to leave their island on account of difficulties with the local church authorities, who were not broad enough to admit the simple sufficiency of Mr. Duncan's lay ministrations. He removed with his people to another island, where they are now living under the protection of the United States flag. In view of the lessons of history, they are likely to undergo a severe trial and considerable demoralization as soon as they mingle freely with the surrounding whites. They have so far developed and enjoyed much of what is best in civilization without its evils and temptations; and whenever one of them does infringe upon their simple but exacting code he is summarily dealt with.

Here is another illustration: In 1869 those Sioux who had been for three years confined in a military prison, on account of the outbreak of 1862, were placed upon a small reservation at Santee, Nebraska. My father was among them. He had thought much, and concluded that reservation life meant practically life imprisonment and death to manhood. He also saw that our wild life was almost at an end; therefore he resolved to grasp the only chance remaining to the red man--namely, to plunge boldly into the white man's life, and swim or die.

With twenty-five or thirty fellow-tribesmen who were of like mind with himself, he set out for the Big Sioux River to take up a homestead like a white man. Far from urging it, Government officials disapproved and discouraged this brave undertaking. The Indians selected a choice location, forty miles above what is now the beautiful little city of Sioux Falls, South Dakota, and here they established the first Sioux citizen community. The post-office was named Flandreau, and formed the nucleus of a large and flourishing town. Remember, this was six years before Sitting Bull and Crazy Horse made their last stand on the Little Big Horn, where they wiped out General Custer's command, the Seventh Cavalry.

This remarkable Indian colony became known far and wide. The Sioux were bona fide homesteaders and met all the requirements of the law. They occupied thirty miles of the finest bottom lands with their timber; except for these wooded river bottoms, the country is all treeless prairie. They were all Presbyterians and devout church-goers. Rev. John P. Williamson was their much-loved missionary; and their church was served for many years by a native pastor--my brother, Rev. John Eastman. Nearly all built good homes. Mr. Williamson says, and Moody County records corroborate the statement, that for twenty years there was not a single crime or misdemeanor recorded against one of these Indians.

As the Big Sioux valley is noted for its fertility, it was not long before the rest of the land was taken up by white farmers. These Indians proved good neighbors. It is told of them that, during the hard years 1873 to 1875, when drought and grasshoppers afflicted the land, they organized a relief society for the benefit of their poorer white neighbors, and in many instances furnished them with cordwood as well as seed-corn and potatoes.

For years the Flandreau Sioux controlled the politics of Moody County, and although after the district had become more thickly settled they lost their numerical preponderance, they still wielded much influence in years when the parties were pretty equally divided. As late as 1898 they held the balance of power, and were accordingly treated with respectful consideration.

From this little Indian community more than one earnest youth has gone forth to work for race and country in a wider field. My father brought me there from wild life in Canada in 1872, and after two years in the little day school he sent me away to master the secret of the white man's power. Only a few years earlier he himself was a wild Sioux warrior, whose ambitions ran wholly along the traditional lines of his people. Who can say that civilization is beyond the reach of the untutored primitive man in a single generation? It did not take my father two thousand years, or ten years, to grasp its essential features; and although he never went to school a day in his life, he lived a broad-minded and self-respecting citizen. It took me about fifteen years to prepare to enter it on the plane of a professional man, and I have stayed with it ever since.

It is noticeable that when the Flandreaus consented to reenter their names on the tribal rolls in order to regain their inheritance, they fell into the claws of the professional politicians, and a degree of demoralization set in. Yet during the early period of free initiative and self-development, some of their best youth had gone out and are now lost in the world at large, in the sense that they are wholly separated from their former life, and are contributing their mite to the common good. Those who remain, as well as other bands of citizen Sioux with whom I am acquainted, are becoming more and more completely identified with the general farming population of Nebraska and the Dakotas.

LEGAL STATUS OF INDIANS

The door to American citizenship has been open to the Indian in general only since the passage of the Dawes severalty act, in 1887. Before that date his status was variously defined as that of a member of an independent foreign nation, of a "domestic dependent nation," as a ward of the Government, or, as some one has wittily said, a "perpetual inhabitant with diminutive rights." The Dawes act conferred upon those who accepted allotments of land in severalty the protection of the courts and all the rights of citizenship, including the suffrage. It also provided that the land thus patented to the individual Indian could not be alienated nor was it taxable for a period of twenty-five years from the date of allotment.

Of the 330,000 Indians in the United States, considerably more than half are now allotted, and 70,000 hold patents in fee. The latest report of the Indian Bureau gives the total number of Indian citizens at about 75,000. Those still living on communal land are being allotted at the rate of about 5,000 a year. The question of taxation of allotments has been a vexed one. Some Indians have hesitated to accept full citizenship because of fear of taxation; while white men living in the vicinity of large Indian holdings have naturally objected to shouldering the entire burden. Yet as the last census shows 73 per cent. of all Indians as taxed and counted toward the population of their Congressional districts, it appears that taxed or taxable Indians are not necessarily citizens; though they must be considered, in the words of Prof. F. A. McKenzie, who compiled the Indian census, as at least "potential citizens."

The so-called "Burke bill" (1906) provides that Indians allotted after that date shall not be declared citizens until after the expiration of the twenty-five-year trust period. This act has served no particular purpose except to further confuse the status of the Indian. The "Carter code bill," now pending in Congress, provides for a commission of experts to codify existing statutes and define this status clearly, and has been strongly endorsed by the Society of American Indians and the Indian Rights Association. It ought to be made law.

There is a special law under which an Indian may apply to be freed from guardianship by proving his ability to manage his own affairs. If his application is approved by the Interior Department, he may then rent or sell his property at will. About five hundred such applications were approved during the fiscal year 1912-13.

The Pueblos and a few other Indians are or may become citizens under special treaty stipulations. The 5,000 New York Indians, although among those longest in contact with civilization, yet because of state treaties and the claims of the Ogden Land Company, still hold their lands in common, and are backward morally and socially. It is likely that the United States will eventually pay the company's claim of $200,000 to free these people. A few of them are well educated and have attained citizenship as individuals by separating themselves from their tribe. Professor McKenzie, who has deeply studied the situation for years, proposes a scheme of progressive advance toward full citizenship, each step to be accompanied by decreasing paternal control: as, for instance: (1) Tribal ward; (2) Allotted ward; (3) Citizen ward; (4) Full citizen.

INDIANS AS POLITICIANS

In almost every state there are some Indian voters, and in South Dakota and Oklahoma there are counties officered and controlled by Indian citizens. It is interesting to note that the citizen Indian is no ignorant or indifferent voter. If he learns and masters anything at all, it is the politics of his county and state. It is a matter of long experience with him, as he has been handled by politicians ever since he entered the reservation, and there is not a political trick that he cannot understand. He is a ready student of human nature, and usually a correct observer. I am sorry to say that the tendency of the new generation is to be diplomats of a lower type, quick and smart, but not always sound. At present, like any crude or partially developed people, politics is their hobby.

Yet there remains a sprinkling of the old Indian type, which is strongly averse to all unfair or underhanded methods; and there are a few of the younger men who combine the best in both standards, and refuse to look upon the new civilization as a great, big grab-bag. It is not strange that a majority are influenced by the prevailing currents of American life. Before they understood the deeper underlying principles of organized society, they had seen what they naturally held to be high official duties and responsibilities ruthlessly bartered and trafficked with before their eyes. They did not realize that this was a period of individual graft and misuse of office for which true civilization was not responsible.

Among the thinking and advanced class of Indians there is, after all, no real bitterness or pessimistic feeling. It has long been apparent to us that absolute distinctions cannot be maintained under the American flag. Yet we think each race should be allowed to retain its own religion and racial codes as far as is compatible with the public good, and should enter the body politic of its own free will, and not under compulsion. This has not been the case with the native American. Everything he stood for was labelled "heathen," "savage," and the devil's own; and he was forced to accept modern civilization in toto against his original views and wishes. The material in him and the method of his reconstruction have made him what he is. He has defied all the theories of the ethnologists. If any one can show me a fair percentage of useful men and women coming out of the jail or poor-house, I will undertake to show him a larger percentage of useful citizens graduating from the pauperizing and demoralizing agency system.

There was no real chance for the average man of my race until the last thirty-five years; and even during that time he has been under the unholy rule of the political boss and "little czar" of the Indian agency, from whose control he is not even yet entirely free. You are suffering from a civic disease, and we are affected by it. When you are cured, and not until then, we may hope to be thoroughly well men.

INHERITANCE AND OTHER FRAUDS

Here is another point of attack for the men who continually hover about the Indian like vultures above a sick or helpless man--the law providing that the allotments of deceased Indians may be sold for the benefit of their legal heirs, even though the time limit of twenty-five years protected title may not have expired. I consider the law a just one, but the work of determining the heirs is complicated and difficult. It is only last year that Congress has appropriated $50,000 for this purpose, although forty thousand inheritance cases are now pending, and much fraud has already been accomplished.

Representative Burke has shown that the bulk of the minors and incompetent Indians in Oklahoma have been swindled out of their property by dishonest administrators and guardians. Hon. Warren K. Moorehead, of the United States Board of Indian Commissioners, who investigated the situation in that state, intimates that as many as 21,000 such cases exist there. He says the handling of estates in Oklahoma costs often from 30 to 90 per cent., whereas the average rate in thirty states is 3 per cent. "Why do not our laws prevent the robbing of Indians? Because they are not enforced," declares Mr. Moorehead, who also investigated White Earth, Minnesota, a few years ago, and uncovered a scandal of large proportions, relating to the theft of over two hundred thousand acres of valuable land, as a result of suddenly removing all restrictions on the mixed bloods at that agency, many of whom were incompetent to manage their own affairs.

Much of this graft might readily be stopped, and the ignorant Indian protected, were it not for the fact that the relationship between the shysters and certain officials is very much like that between the police of New York City and the keepers of illegal resorts. When complaint is made, big envelopes with "U. S." printed in the corner pass back and forth--and that is too often the end of it! The Sioux call the U. S. Indian inspectors, who are supposed to discover and report abuses, "Big Cats"; but an old chief once said to me: "They ought rather to be called prairie owls, who are blind in the daytime and have rattlesnakes for their bedfellows!"

At the suggestion, I believe, of Dr. George Bird Grinnell and Hamlin Garland, an attempt was made under President Roosevelt to systematize the Indian nomenclature. The Indian in his native state bears no surname; and wife and children figuring under entirely different names from that of the head of the family, the law has been unnecessarily embarrassed. I received a special appointment to revise the allotment rolls of the Sioux nation. It was my duty to group the various members of one family under a permanent name, selected for its euphony and appropriateness from among the various cognomens in use among them, of course suppressing mistranslations and grotesque or coarse nicknames calculated to embarrass the educated Indian. My instructions were that the original native name was to be given the preference, if it were short enough and easily pronounced by Americans. If not, a translation or abbreviation might be used, while retaining as much as possible of the distinctive racial flavor. No English surname might be arbitrarily given, but such as were already well established might be retained if the owner so desired. Many such had been unwisely given to children by teachers and missionaries, and in one family I found a George Washington, a Daniel Webster, and a Patrick Henry! The task was quite complicated and there were many doubts and suspicions to overcome, as some feared lest it should be another trick to change the Indian's name after he had been allotted, and so defraud him safely. During the seven years spent in this work,

I came upon many cases of inheritance frauds. In the face of what appear to be iron-clad rules and endless red tape, it is a problem how these things can happen without the knowledge of responsible officials!

THE INDIAN AS HIS OWN ATTORNEY

Some years since an interesting case came up at Standing Rock Agency, N.D., which illustrates the ability of the modern Indian to manage his own affairs when he is permitted to do so. It was proposed to lease nearly the whole reservation, the occupied as well as the unoccupied portion, to two cattle companies, but in order to be legal, the consent of the Indians was necessary. An effort was made to secure their signatures, and interested parties had nearly the requisite two thirds of them fooled, when a mixed blood by the name of Louis Primeau learned of the game, and brought it to the attention of the people.

They made a strong and intelligent resistance, asked for a hearing in Washington and sent on a delegation to present their case. Immediately the agent got up a rival delegation of "good Indians," fed and clothed for the occasion, to contradict the first and declare that the people were willing to sign, all save the "kickers and trouble-makers."

My brother, the Rev. John Eastman, and I were in Washington at the time. The Indian delegation who protested against the leases was given no show at all before the Department, because it appeared that influential Western Senators were upholding the interests of the cattle companies. Primeau came to my brother for help; and we finally secured a hearing before the Senate Committee on Indian Affairs.

It happened to be a Democratic Senate, although a Republican President was in office; and the head of that committee was Senator Stewart of Nevada. Before him the braves fought their unequal battle to a finish. They had their credentials and the minutes of the meeting at which they had been elected, and they stated clearly their people's reasons for opposing the leases-- reasons which were sound on the face of them. They also declared that the Indian Commissioner had sent a telegram to their agent saying that if they would not sign they would be ignored by the Department, and the leases approved without their consent, although such consent was required both by treaty and statute.

It was immediately denied by the other side that any such telegram had been sent, upon which the wily Sioux played their trump card: they produced a certified copy of the dispatch which they had obtained from the operator, and publicly handed this piece of evidence to Senator Stewart.

The Indians also consulted Judge Springer of Illinois, who, after reviewing their case, said that they could serve an injunction on both the Secretary of the Interior and Commissioner, in the District of Columbia. This they did. The officials asked for thirty days; and the Commissioner of Indian Affairs personally hastened to Standing Rock, where he gave the red men a good scolding for their audacity, at the same time telling them that no lease had been made, or would be made.

President Roosevelt then sent Dr. Grinnell, a well-known friend of the Indian, to make an independent investigation. Dr. Grinnell reported that the Walker lease was entirely opposed to the Indians' interests, and that it would not only be unwise, but wrong, to approve it. The Lemmon lease of the unoccupied portion of the reservation was afterward executed with the Indians' consent.

There are innumerable such instances, but this one is worthy of mention because of the spirit and success with which the Indians conducted their own case. Very often their property is dissipated in spite of the fact that there are men among them who fully grasp the situation. These men protest, but it is of no use. They are denounced as "insubordinate," "disturbers of the peace," and worthless prevaricators. Here is where national honor and the rights of a dependent people are sacrificed to the politicians. When we consider that the Indian still owns more than 70,000,000 acres of land, and trust funds stated at $48,000,000, the proceeds of ceded territory, it may be seen that this immense estate largely in the hands of "wards" and illiterate persons presents a very serious problem.

It has come to be more and more the case that the Indian, so long and so oppressively paternalized, is allowed to take a hand in his own development. This is as it should be. Many theories have been advanced concerning him; but I think we all agree that he has outgrown the present method, which now seems to retard his progress. Yet the old machinery continues to exist in cumbersome and more or less inefficient form. It is a question whether it really does much more good than harm; but it seems clear that some of the tribes still need intelligent and honest guardianship. To my mind, this machinery might be adjusted more nearly to the requirements of the present-day Indian.

Professor Moorehead has suggested the plan of putting the Indian Bureau under a commission of several men, to be appointed for long terms or for life, free of political considerations. I can scarcely conceive of wholly non-partisan appointments in this age, but length of service would be a great advantage, and it does seem to me this experiment would be worth trying. Such a commission should have full authority to deal with all Indian matters without reference to any other department. I would add that one half of its members might well be of Indian blood.

CHAPTER VIII

THE INDIAN IN COLLEGE AND THE PROFESSIONS

It is the impression of many people who are not well informed on the Indian situation that book education is of little value to the race, particularly what is known as the higher education. The contrary is true. What we need is not less education, but more; more trained leaders to uphold the standards of civilization before both races. Among Indian college and university graduates a failure is very rare; I am sure I have not met one, and really do not know of one.

The press is responsible for many popular errors. Whenever an Indian indulges in any notorious misbehavior, he is widely heralded as a "Carlisle graduate," although as a matter of fact he may never have attended that famous school, or have been there for a short time only. Obviously the statement is intended to discredit the educated Indian. But Carlisle is not a college or university, although, because of the wonderful athletic prowess of its students, they have met and defeated the athletes of many a white university on the football field. Its curriculum is considerably below that of the ordinary high school; it is a practical or vocational school, giving a fair knowledge of some trade together with the essentials of an English education, but no Latin or other foreign language. Consequently its graduates must attend a higher preparatory school for several years before they can enter college.

It will be seen, then, that the college-educated men and women of my race have accomplished quite a feat, considering their antecedents and wholly foreign point of view. They have had to adjust themselves to a new way of thinking, as well as a new language, before they could master such abstract ideas and problems as are presented by mathematics and the sciences. Their own schools graduate them at a mature age and do not prepare them for college. Furthermore, they are almost always hampered by lack of means. Nevertheless, an increasing number have succeeded in the undertaking.

TRIALS OF THE EDUCATED INDIAN

I wish to contradict the popular misconception that an educated Indian will necessarily meet with strong prejudice among his own people, or will be educated out of sympathy with them. From their point of view, a particularly able or well-equipped man of their race is a public blessing, and all but public property. That was the old rule among us. Up to a very recent period an educated Indian could not succeed materially; he could not better himself, because the people required him to give unlimited free service, according to the old regime. I have even known one to be killed by the continual demands upon him.

There was a time (not so long ago, either) when the educated Indian stood in a very uncomfortable position between his people and the Government officials and shady politicians. Every complaint was brought to him, as a matter of course; and he was expected to expose and redress every wrong. As I have said elsewhere, such efforts are generally useless, and resulted only in damage to his financial position and his reputation. No doubt he often invited attacks upon himself by a rashness born of his ardent sympathy for his fellow-tribesmen. In this matter I speak from personal experience as well as long observation.

Even in the old, wild days, an education was appreciated by the Indians; but it was a hard life for the educated man. They made him carry too heavy a burden, without much recompense save honor and respect. But we have pretty well passed through that period, and the native graduates of our higher institutions have begun to show their strength and enlarge their views. They have not only done well for themselves and their race, but they stand before the world as living illustrations of its capacity, disproving many theories concerning untutored races.

NO "INFERIOR RACE"

It was declared without qualification by the Universal Races Congress at London in 1911 that there is no inherently superior race, therefore no inferior race. From every race some individuals have mastered the same curriculum and passed the same tests, and in some instances members of so-called "uncivilized" races have stood higher than the average "civilized" student; therefore they have the same inherent ability. Certain peoples have remained undeveloped because of their religion, philosophy, and form of government; in other words, because of the racial environment. Change the environment, and the race is transformed. Certainly the American Indian has clearly demonstrated the truth of this assertion.

The very mention of the name "Indian" in earlier days would make the average white man's blood creep with thoughts of the war-whoop and the scalping-knife. A little later it suggested chiefly feathers and paint and "Buffalo Bill's Wild West." To-day the association is rather with the Carlisle school and its famous athletes; but to the thinking mind the name suggests deeper thoughts and higher possibilities.

It was no less a man than Theodore Roosevelt who said to me once in the White House that he would give anything to have a drop of Sioux or Cheyenne blood in his veins. It is a fact that the intelligent and educated Indian has no social prejudice to contend with. His color is not counted against him. He is received cordially and upon equal terms in school, college, and society.

Dr. Booker Washington is in the habit of saying jocosely that the negro blood is the strongest in the world, for one drop of it makes a "nigger" of a white man. I would argue that the Indian blood is even stronger, for a half-blood negro and Indian may pass for an Indian, and so be admitted to first-class hotels and even to high society. All that an Indian needs in order to be popular, and indeed to be lionized if he so desires, is to get an education and hold up his head as a member of the oldest American aristocracy. Many of our leading men have married into excellent families and are prominent in cultivated white communities. We want the best in two races and civilizations in exchange for what we have lost.

Some of us have entered upon every known professional career, such as medicine, law, the ministry, education and the sciences, politics and higher business management, art and literature. It may be well to mention some of our best-known professional men and women. The doctors seem to have been the first to enter the general field in competition with their white colleagues: at first, to be sure, as "Indian herb doctors," or quacks of one sort or another, but later as competent graduated physicians. The Government has utilized several in the Indian service, and others have established themselves in private practice.

SOME NOTED INDIANS OF TO-DAY

Perhaps the foremost of these is Dr. Carlos Montezuma of Chicago, a full-blooded Apache, who was purchased for a few steers while in captivity to the Pimas, who were enemies of his people. He was brought to Chicago by the man who ransomed him, a reporter and photographer, and when his benefactor died, the boy became the protégé of the Chicago Press Club. A large portrait of him adorns the parlor of the club, showing him as the naked Indian captive of about four years old.

He went to the public school, then to Champaign University, Illinois, and from there to the Northwestern University, where he was graduated from the medical department. All this time, although receiving some aid from various sources, he largely supported himself. After graduation Dr. Montezuma was sent by the Government as physician to an Indian agency in Montana, and later transferred to the Carlisle school. In a few years he returned to Chicago and opened an office. He has been a prominent physician there for a number of years, and was recently married to a lady of German descent. He stands uncompromisingly for the total abolition of the reservation system and of the Indian Bureau, holding that the red man must be allowed to work out his own salvation.

One of the earliest practitioners of our race was Dr. Susan La Flesche Picotte of the Omaha tribe. Having prepared at Hampton Institute and elsewhere, she entered the Philadelphia Medical College for Women. When she had finished, she returned to her tribe, and was for some time in the Government service. She has since taken up private practice and also had charge of a mission hospital. Dr. Picotte is a sister of Bright Eyes (Susette La Flesche) and also of Francis La Flesche of Washington, D. C. There is another Indian doctor, not of full blood, who is president of the City Club of Chicago and active in civic reform. In several Middle Western cities there are successful doctors and dentists of my race.

In the profession of law we have none of full blood whose fame is national. Judge Hiram Chase of the Omahas and others have won local distinction. The Hon. Charles Curtis, Senator from Kansas, was a successful lawyer in Topeka when he was elected to the House of Representatives, and later to the United States Senate. His mother is a Kaw Indian. Mr. Curtis was and is a leader of the Republican party in his state. Senator Owen of Oklahoma is part Cherokee. The whole country has come to realize his ability and influence. Representative Carter of Oklahoma is also an Indian.

During my student days in New Hampshire I was often told that Daniel Webster was part Indian on his mother's side. Certainly his physiognomy as well as his unequalled logic corroborated the story. We all know that governors and other men of mark have proclaimed themselves descendants of Pocahontas; I have met several in the West and South. I know that the late Senators Quay of Pennsylvania and Morgan of Alabama had some Indian blood, for they themselves told me so; and I have been told the same of Senators Clapp and La Follette, but have never verified it. Their wonderful aggressiveness and dauntless public service in my mind point to native descent, and if they can truthfully claim it I feel sure that they will be proud to do so. They must know that many distinguished army officers as well as traders and explorers left sons and daughters among the American tribes, especially during the first half of the nineteenth century. As late as 1876 Dr. Washington Mathews, a surgeon in the United States Army, brought down on a Missouri River steamboat a Gros Ventre son, and left him with the missionary teacher, Dr. Alfred L. Riggs, to rear and educate. This military surgeon and scientist not only attained the rank of major-general, but he became one of our foremost archeologists. The boy was called Berthold, from the place of his birth. He was afterward sent to Yankton College, but I do not know what became of him. As for those brilliant men, so many in number, who have the blood of both races in their veins, I will not pretend to claim for the Indian all the credit of their talents and energy.

In the ministry we have many able and devoted men--more than in any other profession. The Presbyterian Church alone has thirty-eight and the Episcopal Church about twenty, with a less number in several other denominations, and two Roman Catholic priests. Most of these labor among their own people, though the Rev. Frank Wright, a Choctaw, is well known as an evangelistic preacher and singer.

One of our best-known clergymen is Rev. Sherman Coolidge, a full-blood Arapahoe. He has had an unusual career, having been taken prisoner as a boy by an officer of the army. He was sent to school and eventually graduated from Bishop Whipple's Seabury Divinity School at Faribault, Minn. Since that time Doctor Coolidge has devoted himself to the Christianization of his race. He is the president of our recently organized Society of American Indians.

Bishop Whipple developed many able preachers, of whom perhaps the most accomplished was the Rev. Charles Smith Cook, of the Yankton Sioux. He was the son of a Sioux woman and a military officer. Mr. Cook was graduated from Trinity College, Hartford, and later from Seabury Divinity School. He had unusual eloquence and personal charm, and became at once one of Bishop Hare's ablest helpers in his great work among the Sioux. Stationed at Pine Ridge at the time of the Wounded Knee massacre, he opened his church to the wounded Indian prisoners as an emergency hospital. His much regretted death occurred a few months later. He was a tireless worker and much loved by his people.

One of our promising young ministers is the Rev. Henry Roe Cloud, a Winnebago, graduated from Yale and Oberlin. Stephen Jones, a Sioux, who was graduated from the Y. M. C. A. training-school at Springfield, Mass., has done good work as field secretary among the Indians for a number of years. I should add that there are many ministers of my race who have no college degree nor much education in the English language, yet who are among our most able and influential leaders. My own brother, Rev. John Eastman, who passed but a short time in school, has not only been a successful preacher among the Sioux but for many years their trusted adviser and representative to look after their interests at the national capital.

A few men and many women have succeeded in the teaching profession, most of them in the United States Indian Service. It is the express policy of the Government to use the educated Indians, whenever possible, in promoting the advancement of their race; indeed some of the treaties include this stipulation. Therefore preference is given them by the Indian Bureau, and although they must pass a civil-service examination to prove their fitness, such examination, in their case, is non-competitive. They have been prepared in the larger Government schools, in many instances with the addition of normal and college courses. At least two are superintendents of schools. A number of young women, Carlisle graduates, have taken up trained nursing as a profession, and are practising successfully both among whites and Indians.

In the sciences, especially in ethnology and archeology, we have several who have rendered material service. William Jones, a Sac and Fox quarter blood, was a graduate of Hampton and of Harvard University. He took post-graduate work at Columbia, and was a pupil of those distinguished scientists, Dr. Putnam and Dr. Boas. The latter has called him one of our ablest archeologists. Dr. Jones travelled among the various tribes, even to the coast of Labrador, and labored assiduously in the cause of science for Harvard and the Marshall Field Museum of Chicago, as well as other institutions. It was the Chicago Museum which sent him to the Philippine Islands, where he was murdered by the natives a few years ago.

We have also such men as Professor Hewitt of the Smithsonian Institution, Francis La Flesche of the same, and Arthur C. Parker of Albany, N. Y., who is state archeologist.

In literature several writers of Indian blood have appeared during the past few years, and have won a measure of recognition. Francis La Flesche, an Omaha, has collaborated with Miss Alice C. Fetcher in ethnological work, and is also the author of a pleasing story of life in an Indian school called "The Middle Five." Zitkalasa, a Sioux (now Mrs. Bonney), attended a Western college, where she distinguished herself in an intercollegiate oratorical contest. Soon afterward she appeared in the Atlantic Monthly as the writer of several papers of an autobiographical nature, which attracted favorable attention, and were followed by a little volume of Indian legends and several short stories. Mrs. Bonney has more recently written the book of an Indian opera called "The Sun Dance," which has been produced in Salt Lake City by university students. John Oskinson, a Cherokee, was first heard of as the winner in an intercollegiate literary contest, and he is now on the staff of Collier's Weekly. The Five Civilized Nations of Oklahoma can show many other writers and journalists.

In higher business lines a number have shown special ability. General Pleasant Porter, who died recently, was president of a short railroad line in Oklahoma; Mr. Hill, of Texas, is reputed to be a millionaire; Howard Gansworth, a graduate of Carlisle and Princeton, is a successful business man in Syracuse, N. Y.; and many of more or less Indian blood have gone forth into the world to do business on a large scale.

In the athletic world this little race has no peer, as is sufficiently proven by their remarkable record in football, baseball, and track athletics. A few years ago I asked that good friend of the Indian, Gen. R. H. Pratt, why he did not introduce football in his school. "Why," said he, "if I did that, half the press of the country would attack me for developing the original war instincts and savagery of the Indian! The public would be afraid to come to our games!"

"Major," I said, "that is exactly why I want you to do it. We will prove that the Indian is a gentleman and a sportsman; he will not complain; he will do nothing unfair or underhand; he will play the game according to the rules, and will not swear--at least not in public!"

Not long afterward the game was introduced at Carlisle, and I was asked by the General to visit Montana and the Dakotas to secure pupils for the school, and, incidentally, recruits for his football warriors. The Indians' victory was complete. These boys always fight the battle on its own merits; they play a clean game, and lose very few games during the season, although they meet all our leading universities, each on its own home grounds.

From the fleet Deerfoot to this day we boast the noted names of Longboat, Sockalexis, Bemus Pierce, Frank Hudson, Tewanima, Metoxen, Myers, Bender, and Jim Thorpe. Thorpe is a graduate of the Carlisle school, and at the

Olympic Games in Sweden in 1912 he won the title of the greatest all-round athlete in the world.

PROBLEMS OF RACE LEADERSHIP

I have been asked why my race has not produced a Booker Washington. There are many difficulties in the way of efficient race leadership; one of them is the large number of different Indian tribes with their distinct languages, habits, and traditions, and with old tribal jealousies and antagonisms yet to be overcome. Another, and a more serious obstacle, is the dependent position of the Indian, and the almost arbitrary power in the hands of the Indian Bureau.

About fifteen years ago the idea of a national organization of progressive Indians was discussed at some length by Rev. Sherman Coolidge, my brother, John Eastman, and myself. At that time we concluded that the movement would not be understood either by our own race or the American people in general, and that there was grave danger of arousing the antagonism of the Bureau. If such a society were formed, it would necessarily take many problems of the race under consideration, and the officials at Washington and in the field are sensitive to criticism, nor are they accustomed to allowing the Indian a voice in his own affairs. Furthermore, many of the most progressive red men are enlisted in the Government service, which would make their position a very difficult one in case of any friction with the authorities. Very few Indians are sufficiently independent of the Bureau to speak and act with absolute freedom.

Some ten years later I was called to Columbus, Ohio, to lecture for the Ohio State University on the same course with Dr. Coolidge and Dr. Montezuma. Prof. F. A. McKenzie of the university arranged the course, and soon afterward he wrote me that he believed the time was now ripe to organize our society. We corresponded with leading Indians and arranged a meeting at Columbus for the following April. At this meeting five were present besides myself: Dr. Montezuma, Thomas Sloan, Charles E. Dagenett, Henry Standingbear, and Miss Laura Cornelius. We organized as a committee, and issued a general call for a conference in October at the university, upon the cordial invitation of Dr. McKenzie and President Thompson.

Four annual conferences have now been held, and the fifth is announced for next October at Oklahoma City. The society has 500 active and about the same number of associate members; the latter are white friends of the race who are in sympathy with our objects. Our first president is Rev. Sherman Coolidge, and Arthur C. Parker is secretary and treasurer. The Society of American Indians issues a quarterly journal devoted to the proceedings of the conferences and the interests of the Indian race. At these meetings and in this journal various phases of our situation have been intelligently and courageously discussed, and certain remedies have been suggested for the evils brought to light. These debates should at least open the public ear.

Of course the obstacles to complete success that I have referred to still exist, and there are others as well. Our people have not been trained to work together harmoniously. It is a serious question what principles we should stand for and what line of work we ought to undertake. Should we devote ourselves largely to exposing the numerous frauds committed upon Indians? Or should we keep clear of these matters, avoid discussion of official methods and action, and simply aim at arousing racial pride and ambition along new lines, holding up a modern ideal for the support and encouragement of our youth? Should we petition Congress and in general continue along the lines of the older Indian associations? Or should we rather do intensive work among our people, looking especially toward their moral and social welfare?

I stand for the latter plan. Others think differently; and, as a matter of fact, a Washington office has been opened and much attention paid to governmental affairs. It is a large task. The declared objects of the society, in almost the words originally chosen by its six founders, are as follows:

OBJECTS OF THE SOCIETY OF AMERICAN INDIANS

First. To promote and cooperate with all efforts looking to the advancement of the Indian in enlightenment which leave him free, as a man, to develop according to the natural laws of social evolution.

Second. To provide through our open conferences the means for a free discussion on all subjects bearing on the welfare of the race.

Third. To present in a just light the true history of the race, to preserve its records and emulate its distinguishing virtues.

Fourth. To promote citizenship and to obtain the rights thereof.

Fifth. To establish a legal department to investigate Indian problems and to suggest and to obtain remedies.

Sixth. To exercise the right to oppose any movement that may be detrimental to the race.

Seventh. To direct its energies exclusively to general principles and universal interests, and not allow itself to be used for any personal or private interest. The honor of the race and the good of the country shall be paramount.

CHAPTER IX

THE INDIAN'S HEALTH PROBLEM

The physical decline and alarming death-rate of the American Indian of to-day is perhaps the most serious and urgent of the many problems that confront him at the present time. The death-rate is stated by Government officials at about thirty per thousand of the population--double the average rate among white Americans. From the same source we learn that about 70,000 Indians in the United States are suffering from trachoma, a serious and contagious eye disease, and probably 30,000 have tuberculosis in some form. The death-rate from tuberculosis is almost three times that among the whites.

These are grave facts, and cause deep anxiety to the intelligent Indian and to the friends of the race. Some hold pessimistic views looking to its early extinction; but these are not warranted by the outlook, for in spite of the conditions named, the last three census show a slight but continuous increase in the total number of Indians. Nor is this increase among mixed-bloods alone; the full-blooded Indians are also increasing in numbers. This indicates that the race has reached and passed the lowest point of its decline, and is beginning slowly but surely to recuperate.

THE CHANGE TO RESERVATION LIFE

The health situation on the reservations was undoubtedly even worse twenty years ago than it is to-day, but at that period little was heard and still less done about it. It is well known that the wild Indian had to undergo tremendous and abrupt changes in his mode of living. He suffered severely from an indoor and sedentary life, too much artificial heat, too much clothing, impure air, limited space, indigestible food--indigestible because he did not know how to prepare it, and in itself poor food for him. He was compelled often to eat diseased cattle, mouldy flour, rancid bacon, with which he drank large quantities of strong coffee. In a word, he lived a squalid life, unclean and apathetic physically, mentally, and spiritually.

This does not mean all Indians--a few, like the Navajoes, have retained their native vigor and independence--I refer to the typical "agency Indian" of the Northwest. He drove ten to sixty miles to the agency for food; every week-end at some agencies, at others every two weeks, and at still others once a month. This was all the real business he had to occupy him--travelling between cabin and agency warehouses for twenty-five years! All this time he was brooding over the loss of his freedom, his country rich in game, and all the pleasures and satisfactions of wild life. Even the arid plains and wretched living left him he was not sure of, judging from past experience with a government that makes a solemn treaty guaranteeing him a certain territory "forever," and taking it away from him the next year if it appears that some of their own people want it, after all.

Like the Israelites in bondage, our own aborigines have felt the sweet life-giving air of freedom change to the burning heat of a desert as dreary as that of Egypt under Pharaoh. It was during this period of hopeless resignation, gloomily awaiting--what, no Indian could even guess--that his hardy, yet sensitive, organization gave way. Who can wonder at it? His home was a little, one-roomed log cabin, about twelve by twenty feet, mud-chinked, containing a box stove and a few sticks of furniture. The average cabin has a dirt floor and a dirt roof. They are apt to be overheated in winter, and the air is vitiated at all times, but especially at night, when there is no ventilation whatever. Families of four to ten persons lived, and many still live, in these huts. Fortunately the air of the plains is dry, or we should have lost them all!

Remember, these people were accustomed to the purest of air and water.

The teepee was little more than a canopy to shelter them from the elements; it was pitched every few days upon new, clean ground. Clothing was loose and simple, and frequent air and sun baths, as well as baths in water and steam, together with the use of emollient oils, kept the skin in perfect condition. Their food was fresh and wholesome, largely wild meat and fish, with a variety of wild fruits, roots, and grain, and some cultivated ones. At first they could not eat the issue bacon, and on ration days one might see these strips of unwholesome-looking fat lying about on the ground where they had been thrown on the return trip. Flour, too, was often thrown away before the women had learned to make bread raised with cheap baking-powder and fried in grease. But the fresh meat they received was not enough to last until the next ration day. There was no end of bowel trouble when they were forced by starvation to swallow the bacon and ill-prepared bread. Water, too, was generally hauled from a distance with much labor, and stood about in open buckets or barrels for several days.

As their strength waned, they made more fire in the stove and sat over it, drinking rank coffee and tea that had boiled all day on the same stove. After perspiring thus for hours, many would go out into the bitter cold of a Dakota winter with little or no additional clothing, and bronchitis and pneumonia were the inevitable result. The uncured cases became chronic and led straight to tuberculosis in its various forms.

Furthermore, the Indian had not become in any sense immune to disease, and his ignorance placed no check upon contagion and infection. Even the simpler children's diseases, such as measles, were generally fatal. The death-rate of children under five was terrific. I have known women to bear families of six or eight or ten children, and outlive them all, most dying in infancy. In their state of deep depression disease had its golden opportunity, and there seemed to be no escape. What was there to save the race from annihilation within a few years? Nothing, save its heritage of a superb physique and a wonderful patience.

THE INDIAN SERVICE PHYSICIAN

The doctors who were in the service in those days had an easy time of it. They scarcely ever went outside of the agency enclosure, and issued their pills and compounds after the most casual inquiry. As late as 1890, when the

Government sent me out as physician to ten thousand Ogallalla Sioux and Northern Cheyennes at Pine Ridge Agency, I found my predecessor still practising his profession through a small hole in the wall between his office and the general assembly room of the Indians. One of the first things I did was to close that hole; and I allowed no man to diagnose his own trouble or choose his pills. I told him I preferred to do that myself; and I insisted upon thoroughly examining my patients. It was a revelation to them, but they soon appreciated the point, and the demand for my services doubled and trebled.

As no team was provided for my use to visit my patients on a reservation nearly a hundred miles square (or for any other agency doctor at the time), I bought a riding horse, saddle and saddle-bags, and was soon on the road almost day and night. A night ride of fifty to seventy-five miles was an ordinary occurrence; and even a Dakota blizzard made no difference, for I never refused to answer a call. Before many months I was supplied by the Government with a covered buggy and two good horses.

I found it necessary to buy, partly with my own funds and partly with money contributed by generous friends, a supply of suitable remedies as well as a full set of surgical instruments. The drugs supplied by contractors to the Indian service were at that period often obsolete in kind, and either stale or of the poorest quality. Much of my labor was wasted, moreover, because of the impossibility of seeing that my directions were followed, and of securing proper nursing and attention. Major operations were generally out of the question on account of the lack of hospital facilities, as well as the prejudice of the people, though I did operate on several of the severely injured after the massacre at Wounded Knee. In many cases it was my task to supply my patients with suitable food and other necessaries, and my wife was always prepared for a raid on her kitchen and storeroom for bread, soup, sheets, and bandages.

The old-time "medicine-man" was really better than the average white doctor in those days, for although his treatment was largely suggestive, his herbs were harmless and he did allay some distress which the other aggravated, because he used powerful drugs almost at random and did not attend to his cases intelligently. The native practitioners were at first suspicious of me as a dangerous rival, but we soon became good friends, and they sometimes came frankly to me for advice and even proposed to borrow some of my remedies.

Of course, even in that early period when the average Government doctor feared to risk his life by going freely among the people (though there was no real danger unless he invited it), there were a few who were sincere and partially successful, especially some military surgeons.

Now that stage of the medical work among the Indians is past, and the agency doctor has no valid excuse for failing to perform his professional duty. It is true that he is poorly paid and too often overworked; but the equipment is better and there is intelligent supervision. At Pine Ridge, where I labored single-handed, there are now three physicians, with a hospital to aid them in their work. To-day there are two hundred physicians, with a head supervisor and a number of specialists, seventy nurses, and eighty field matrons in the Indian service.

SOME MISTAKES AND THE REMEDIES

Another serious mistake has been made in the poor sanitary equipment of Indian schools. Close confinement and long hours of work were for these children of the forest and plains unnatural and trying at best. Dormitories especially have been shamefully overcrowded, and undesirable pupils, both by reason of disease and bad morals, allowed to mingle freely with the healthy and innocent. Serious mishaps have occurred which have given some of these schools a bad name; but I really believe that greater care is being taken at the present time. It was chiefly at an early period of the Indian's advance toward civilization that both mismanagement and adverse circumstance, combined with his own inexperience and ignorance of the new ways, weakened his naturally splendid powers and paved the way for his present physical decline. His mental lethargy and want of ambition under the deadening reservation system have had much to do with the outcome.

He was in a sense muzzled. He was told: "You are yet a child. You cannot teach your own children, nor judge of their education. They must not even use their mother tongue. I will do it all myself. I have got to make you over; meanwhile, I will feed and clothe you. I will be your nurse and guardian."

This is what happened to this proud and self-respecting race! But since then they have silently studied the world's history and manners; they have wandered far and wide and observed life for themselves. They have thought much. The great change has come about; the work has been done, whether poorly or otherwise, and, upon the whole, the good will prevail. The pessimist may complain that nothing has come of all the effort made in behalf of the Indian. I say that it is not too late for the original American to regain and re 雜 tablish his former physical excellency. Why should he not? Much depends upon his own mental attitude, and this is becoming more normal as the race approaches and some part of it attains to self-support and full citizenship. As I have said, conditions are improving; yet much remains to be done; and it should be done quickly. An exhaustive inquiry into health conditions among the tribes was made in accordance with an act of Congress in 1912, and the report presented in January, 1913, was in brief as follows:

1. Trachoma is exceedingly prevalent among Indians.

2. Tuberculosis among Indians is greatly in excess of that estimated for the white population.

3. The sanitary conditions upon reservations are, on the whole, bad.

4. The primitive Indian requires instruction in personal hygiene and habits of living in stationary dwellings.

5. The sanitary conditions in most Indian schools are unsatisfactory.

6. There is danger of the spread of tuberculosis and trachoma from the Indian to other races.

7. Due care is not taken in the collection and preservation of vital statistics.

8. The medical department of the Indian Bureau is hampered by insufficient authority and inadequate compensation.

As a result of this and other investigations, increased appropriations have been asked for, and to a limited extent provided, for the purpose of preventing and treating disease, and especially of checking the spread of serious contagious ailments. More stress is being laid upon sanitary precautions and hygienic instruction in Indian schools, and an effort is made to carry this instruction into the Indian home through field matrons and others. Four sanatoria or sanitarium schools have been successfully established in suitable climates, and it is recommended by an Indian Service specialist that certain boarding-school plants be set apart for trachoma pupils, where they can have thorough and consistent treatment and remain until the cure is complete. Much larger appropriations are needed in order to carry out in full these beneficent measures, and I earnestly hope that they may be forthcoming.

It is interesting to note that whereas a few years ago the Indians were reproved for placing their sick in canvas tents and arbors, and in every way discouraged from any attempt to get out of their stifling houses into the life-giving air, sleeping-porches are now being added to their hospitals, and open-air schools and sanatoria established for their children. The world really does move, and to some extent it seems to be moving round to his original point of view. It is not too late to save his physique as well as his unique philosophy, especially at this moment when the spirit of the age has recognized the better part of his scheme of life.

It is too late, however, to save his color; for the Indian young men themselves have entirely abandoned their old purpose to keep aloof from the racial melting-pot. They now intermarry extensively with Americans and are rearing a healthy and promising class of children. The tendency of the mixed-bloods is toward increased fertility and beauty as well as good mentality. This cultivation and infusion of new blood has relieved and revived the depressed spirit of the first American to a noticeable degree, and his health problem will be successfully met if those who are entrusted with it will do their duty.

My people have a heritage that can be depended upon, and the two races at last in some degree understand one another. I have no serious concern about the new Indian, for he has now reached a point where he is bound to be recognized. This is his native country, and its affairs are vitally his affairs, while his well-being is equally vital to his white neighbors and fellow-Americans.

CHAPTER X

NATIVE ARTS AND INDUSTRIES

In his sense of the 鉦 thetic, which is closely akin to religious feeling, the American Indian stands alone. In accord with his nature and beliefs, he does not pretend to imitate the inimitable, or to reproduce exactly the work of the Great Artist. That which is beautiful must not be trafficked with, but must only be reverenced and adored. It must appear in speech and action. The symmetrical and graceful body must express something of it. Beauty, in our eyes, is always fresh and living, even as God Himself dresses the world anew at each season of the year.

It may be artistic to imitate nature and even try to improve upon her, but we Indians think it very tiresome, especially as one considers the material side of the work--the pigment, the brush, the canvas! There is no mystery there; you know all about them! Worst of all is the commercialization of art. The rudely carved totem pole may appear grotesque to the white man, but it is the sincere expression of the faith and personality of the Indian craftsman, and has never been sold or bartered until it reached civilization.

THE INDIAN'S VIEWPOINT

Now we see at once the root of the red man's failure to approach even distantly the artistic standard of the civilized world. It lies not in the lack of creative imagination--for in this quality he is a born artist--it lies rather in his point of view. I once showed a party of Sioux chiefs the sights of Washington, and endeavored to impress them with the wonderful achievements of civilization. After visiting the Capitol and other famous buildings, we passed through the Corcoran Art Gallery, where I tried to explain how the white man valued this or that painting as a work of genius and a masterpiece of art.

"Ah!" exclaimed an old man, "such is the strange philosophy of the white man! He hews down the forest that has stood for centuries in its pride and grandeur, tears up the bosom of mother earth, and causes the silvery watercourses to waste and vanish away. He ruthlessly disfigures God's own pictures and monuments, and then daubs a flat surface with many colors, and praises his work as a masterpiece!"

This is the spirit of the original American. He holds nature to be the measure of consummate beauty, and its destruction as sacrilege. I have seen in our midsummer celebrations cool arbors built of fresh-cut branches for council and dance halls, while those who attended decked themselves with leafy boughs, carrying shields and fans of the same, and even making wreaths for their horses' necks. But, strange to say, they seldom made a free use of flowers. I once asked the reason of this.

"Why," said one, "the flowers are for our souls to enjoy; not for our bodies to wear. Leave them alone and they will live out their lives and reproduce themselves as the Great Gardener intended. He planted them: we must not pluck them, for it would be selfish to do so."

Indian beadwork in leaf and flower designs is generally modern. The old-time patterns are for the most part simple geometrical figures, which are decorative and emblematic rather than imitative. Shafts of light and shadow alternating or dovetailed represent life, its joys and sorrows. The world is conceived of as rectangular and flat, and is represented by a square. The sky is concave--a hollow sphere. A drawing of the horizon line colored pale yellow stands for dawn; colored red, for sunset. Day is blue, and night black spangled with stars. Lightning, rain, wind, water, mountains, and many other natural features or elements are symbolized rather than copied literally upon many sorts of Indian handiwork. Animal figures are drawn in such a manner as to give expression to the type or spirit of the animal rather than its body, emphasizing the head with the horns, or any distinguishing feature. These designs have a religious significance and furnish the individual with his personal and clan emblem, or coat of arms.

Symbolic decorations are used on blankets, baskets, pottery, and garments of ceremony to be worn at rituals and public functions. Sometimes a man's teepee is decorated in accordance with the standing of the owner. Weapons of war are adorned with emblems, and also pipes, or calumets, but not the every-day weapons used in hunting. The war steed is decorated equally with his rider, and sometimes wears the feathers that signify degrees of honor.

THE WOMAN AND HER CRAFTSMANSHIP

In his weaving, painting, and embroidery of beads and quills the red man has shown a marked color sense, and his blending of brilliant hues is subtle and

Oriental in effect. The women did most of this work and displayed vast ingenuity in the selection of native materials and dyes. A variety of beautiful grasses, roots, and barks are used for baskets by the different tribes, and some even used gorgeous feathers for extra ornamentation. Each was perfectly adapted in style, size, and form to its intended use.

Pottery was made by the women of the Southwest for household furniture and utensils, and their vessels, burned in crude furnaces, were often gracefully shaped and exquisitely decorated. The designs were both imprinted on the soft clay and modeled in relief. The nomadic tribes of the plains could not well carry these fragile wares with them on their wanderings, and accordingly their dishes were mainly of bark and wood, the latter sometimes carved. Spoons were prettily made of translucent horn. They were fond of painting their rawhide cases in brilliant colors. The most famous blankets are made by the Navajoes upon rude hand looms and are wonderfully fine in weave, color, and design.

This native skill combined with love of the work and perfect sincerity--the qualities which still make the Indian woman's blanket or basket or bowl or moccasins of the old type so highly prized--are among the precious things lost or sacrificed to the advance of an alien civilization. Cheap machine-made garments and utensils, without beauty or durability, have crowded out the old; and where the women still ply their ancient trade, they do it now for money, not for love, and in most cases use modern materials and patterns, even imported yarns and "Diamond dyes!" Genuine curios or antiques are already becoming very rare, except in museums, and sometimes command fabulous prices. As the older generation passes, there is danger of losing altogether the secret of Indian art and craftsmanship.

MODERN INDIAN ART

Struck by this danger, and realizing the innate charm of the work and its adaptability to modern demands, a few enthusiasts have made of late years an effort to preserve and extend it, both in order that a distinctive and vitally American art-form may not disappear, and as a means of self-support for Indian women. Depots or stores have been established at various points for the purpose of encouraging such manufactures and of finding a market for them, not so much from commercial as from artistic and philanthropic motives. The best known, perhaps, is the Mohonk Lodge, Colony, Oklahoma, founded under the auspices of the Mohonk Indian Conference, where all work is guaranteed of genuine Indian make, and, as far as possible, of native material and design. Such articles as bags, belts, and moccasins are, however, made in modern form so as to be appropriate for wear by the modern woman. Miss Josephine Foard assisted the women of the Laguna pueblo to glaze their wares, thereby rendering them more salable; and the Indian Industries League, with headquarters in Boston, works along similar lines.

The Indian Bureau reports that over $600,000 worth of Navajo blankets were made during the last year, and that prizes will be awarded this fall for the best blankets made of native wool. At Pima $15,000 worth of baskets and $5,000 worth of pottery was made and sold, and a less amount was produced at several other agencies.

Another modern development, significant of the growing appreciation of what is real and valuable in primitive culture, is the instruction of the younger generation in the Government schools in the traditional arts and crafts of their people. As schooling is compulsory between the ages of six and sixteen years, and from the more distant boarding-schools the pupils are not even allowed to go home for the summer vacation, most of them would otherwise grow up in ignorance of their natural heritage, in legend, music, and art forms as well as practical handicrafts. The greatest difficulty in the way is the finding of competent and sympathetic teachers.

At Carlisle there are and have been for some years two striking exemplars of the native talent and modern culture of their race, in joint charge of the department of Indian art. Angel DeCora was a Winnebago girl, who was graduated from the Hampton school and from the art department of Smith College. She was afterward a pupil of the famous American illustrator, Howard Pyle, and herself made a distinctive success in this field, having illustrated several books and articles on Indian subjects. Some of her work has appeared in Harper's Magazine and other high-class periodicals. She had a studio in New York City for several years, until invited to teach art at the Carlisle school, where she has been ever since.

A few years ago she married William Dietz (Lone Star), who is half Sioux. He is a fine, manly fellow, who was for years a great football player, as well as an accomplished artist. The couple have not only the artistic and poetic temperament in full measure, but they have the pioneer spirit and aspire to do much for their race. The effective cover designs and other art work of the Carlisle school magazine, The Red Man, are the work of Mr. and Mrs. Dietz, who are successfully developing native talent in the production of attractive and salable rugs, blankets, and silver jewelry. Besides this, they are seeking to discover latent artistic gifts among the students in order that they may be fully trained and utilized in the direction of pure or applied art. It is admitted that the average Indian child far surpasses the average white child in this direction. The Indian did not paint nature, not because he did not feel it, but because it was sacred to him. He so loved the reality that he could not venture upon the imitation. It is now time to unfold the resources of his genius, locked up for untold ages by the usages and philosophy of his people. They held it sacrilege to reproduce the exact likeness of the human form or face. This is the reason that early attempts to paint the natives were attended with difficulty, and there are still Indians who refuse to be photographed.

MUSIC, DANCING, DRAMATIC ART

A form of self-expression which has always been characteristic of my race is found in their music. In music is the very soul of the Indian; yet the civilized nations have but recently discovered that such a thing exists! His chants are simple, expressive, and haunting in quality, and voice his inmost feelings, grave or gay, in every emotion and situation in life. They vary much with tribes and even with individuals. A man often composes his own song, which belongs to him and is deeply imbued with his personality. These songs are frequently without words, the meaning being too profound for words; they are direct emanations of the human spirit. If words are used, they are few and symbolic in character. There is no definite harmony in the songs--only rhythm and melody, and there are striking variations of time and intonation which render them difficult to the "civilized" ear.

Nevertheless, within the last few years there has been a serious effort to collect these wild folksongs of the woods and plains by means of notation and the phonograph, and in some cases this has been connected with the attempt to harmonize and popularize them. Miss Alice C. Fletcher, the distinguished ethnologist and student of early American culture, was a pioneer in this field, in which she was assisted by Prof. J. C. Filmore, who is no longer living.

Frederick Burton died several years ago, immediately after the publication of his interesting work on the music of the Ojibways, which is fully illustrated with songs collected and in some instances harmonized by himself. Miss Natalie Curtis devoted much patient study to the songs of the tribes, especially of the Pueblos, and later comers in this field are Farwell, Troyer, Lieurance, and Cadman, the last of whom uses the native airs as a motive for more elaborated songs. His "Land of the Sky Blue Water" is charming, and already very popular. Harold A. Loring of North Dakota has recently harmonized some of the songs of the Sioux.

Several singers of Indian blood are giving public recitals of this appealing and mysterious music of their race. There has even been an attempt to teach it to our schoolchildren, and Geoffrey O'Hara, a young composer of New York City, made a beginning in this direction under the auspices of the Indian Bureau. Native melodies have also been adapted and popularized for band and orchestra by native musicians, of whom the best known are Dennison Wheelock and his brother James Wheelock, Oneidas and graduates of Carlisle. When we recall that as recent as twenty years ago all native art was severely discountenanced and discouraged, if not actually forbidden, in Government schools, and often by missionaries as well, the present awakening is matter for mutual congratulations.

Many Americans have derived their only personal knowledge of Indians from the circus tent and the sawdust arena. The red man is a born actor, a dancer and rider of surpassing agility, but he needs the great out of doors for his stage. In pageantry, and especially equestrian pageantry, he is most effective. His extraordinarily picturesque costume, and the realistic manner in which he illustrates and reproduces the life of the early frontier, has made of him a great, romantic, and popular attraction not only here but in Europe. Several white men have taken advantage of this fact to make their fortunes, of whom the most enterprising and successful was Col. William Cody, better known as "Buffalo Bill."

The Indians engaged to appear in his and other shows have been paid moderate salaries and usually well treated, though cases have arisen in which they have been stranded at long distances from home. As they cannot be taken from the reservation without the consent of the authorities, repeated efforts have been made by missionaries and others to have such permission refused on the ground of moral harm to the participants in these sham battles and dances. Undoubtedly they see a good deal of the seamy side of civilization; but, on the other hand, their travels have proved of educational value, and in some instances opened their eyes to good effect to the superior power of the white man. Sitting Bull and other noted chiefs have, at one time or another, been connected with Indian shows.

A pageant-play based on Longfellow's poem of "Hiawatha" has been given successfully for several years by native Ojibway actors; and individuals of Indian blood have appeared on the stage in minor parts, and more prominently in motion pictures, where they are often engaged to represent tribal customs and historical events.

USEFUL ARTS AND INVENTIONS

Among native inventions which have been of conspicuous use and value to the dispossessors of the Indian we recollect at once the bark canoe, the snowshoe, the moccasin (called the most perfect footwear ever invented), the game of lacrosse and probably other games, also the conical teepee which served as a model for the Sibley army tent. Pemmican, a condensed food made of pounded dried meat combined with melted fat and dried fruits, has been largely utilized by recent polar explorers.

The art of sugar making from the sap of the hard or sugar maple was first taught by the aborigines to the white settlers. In my day the Sioux used also the box elder for sugar making, and from the birch and ash is made a dark-colored sugar that was used by them as a carrier in medicine. However, none of these yield as freely as the maple. The Ojibways of Minnesota still make and sell delicious maple sugar, put up in "mococks," or birch-bark packages. Their wild rice, a native grain of remarkably fine flavor and nutritious qualities, is also in a small way an article of commerce. It really ought to be grown on a large scale and popularized as a package cereal. A large fortune doubtless awaits the lucky exploiter of this distinctive "breakfast food."

In agriculture the achievements of the Indian have probably been underestimated, although it is well known that the Indian corn was the mother of all the choice varieties which to-day form an important source of food supply for the civilized world. The women cultivated the maize with primitive implements, and prepared it for food in many attractive forms, including hominy and succotash, of which the names, as well as the dishes themselves, are borrowed from the red man. He has not always been rewarded in kind for his goodly gifts. In 1830 the American Fur Company established a distillery at the mouth of the Yellowstone River, and made alcohol from the corn raised by the Gros Ventre women, with which they demoralized the men of the Dakotas, Montana, and British Columbia. Besides maize and tobacco, some tribes, especially in the South, grew native cotton and a variety of fruits and vegetables.

The buckskin clothing of my race was exceedingly practical as well as handsome, and has been adapted to the use of hunters, explorers, and frontiersmen, down to the present day. His feathers and other decorations are imitated by women of fashion, and his moccasin was never so much in vogue as now. The old wooden Indian in front of the tobacco store looks less lonely as he gazes upon a procession of bright-eyed young people, with now and then one older, Indian-clad, joyous, and full of health, returning, if only for a few short weeks, to the life he knew of old.

CHAPTER XI

THE INDIAN'S GIFTS TO THE NATION

What does the original American contribute, in the final summing up, to the country of his birth and his adoption? Not much, perhaps, in comparison with the brilliant achievements of civilization; yet, after all, is there not something worthy of perpetuation in the spirit of his democracy--the very essence of patriotism and justice between man and man? Silently, by example only, in wordless patience, he holds stoutly to his native vision. We must admit that the tacit influence of his philosophy has been felt at last, and a self-seeking world has paused in its mad rush to pay him a tribute.

Yes, the world has recognized his type, seized his point of view. We have lived to see monuments erected to his memory. The painter, sculptor, author, scientist, preacher, all have found in him a model worthy of study and serious presentation. Lorado Taft's colossal "Black Hawk" stands wrapped in his stony blanket upon the banks of the Rock River; while the Indian is to keep company with the Goddess of Liberty in New York Harbor, besides many other statues of him which pre-eminently adorn the public parks and halls of our cities.

No longer does the red man live alone in the blood-curdling pages of the sensational story-writer. He is the subject of profound study as a man, a philosopher, a noble type both physically and spiritually. Symmetrical and finely poised in body, the same is true of his character. He stands naked before you, scorning the garb of deception and pretence, for he is a true child of nature.

How has he contributed to the world's progress? By his personal faithfulness to duty and devotion to a trust. He has not advertised his faithfulness nor made capital of his honor. Again and again he has proved his worth as a citizen of his country and of the world by his constancy in the face of hardship and death. Racial antagonism was to him no excuse for breaking his word. This simplicity and fairness has cost him dear; it cost his country and his freedom, even the extinction of his race as a separate and peculiar people; but as a type, an ideal, he lives and will live!

The red man's genius for military tactics and strategy has been admitted again and again by those who have fought against him, often unwillingly, because they saw that he was in the right. His long, unequal struggle against the dominant race has produced a brilliant array of notable men without education in letters. Such were King Philip of the Wampanoags; Pontiac, the great Ottawa; Cornplanter of the Senecas, in the eighteenth century; while in the first half of the nineteenth we have Weatherford of the Creeks, Tecumseh of the Shawnees, Little Turtle of the Miamis, Wabashaw and Wanatan of the Sioux, Black Hawk of the Foxes, Osceola of the Seminoles. During the last half of the century there arose another set of Indian leaders, the last of their type--such men as Ouray of the Utes, Geronimo of the Apaches, Red Cloud, Spotted Tail, and Sitting Bull of the Sioux, Chief Joseph of the Nez Perces, and Dull Knife of the Northern Cheyennes. Men like these are an ornament to any country.

It has been said that their generalship was equal to that of C鏔ar or Napoleon; even greater considering that here was no organization, no treasury, or hope of spoils, or even a stable government behind them. They displayed their leadership under conditions in which Napoleon would have failed. As regards personal bravery, no man could outdo them. After Jackson had defeated the Creeks, he demanded of them the war chief Weatherford, dead or alive. The following night Weatherford presented himself alone at the general's tent, saying: "I am Weatherford; do as you please with me. I would be still fighting you had I the warriors to fight with; but they no longer answer my call, for they are dead."

Chief Joseph, who conducted that masterly retreat of eleven hundred miles, burdened with his women and children, the old men and the wounded, surrendered at last, as he told me in Washington, because he could "bear no longer the sufferings of the innocent." These men were not bloodthirsty or wanton murderers; they were as gentle at home as they were terrific in battle. Chief Joseph would never harm a white woman or child, and more than once helped non-combatants to a place of safety.

In oratory and unstudied eloquence the American Indian has at times equalled even the lofty flights of the Greeks and Romans. The noted Red Jacket, perhaps the greatest orator and philosopher of primitive America, was declared by the late Governor Clinton of New York to be the equal of Demosthenes. President Jefferson called the best-known speech of Logan, the Mingo chief, the "height of human utterance."

Now let us consider some of his definite contributions to the birth and nurture of the United States. We have borrowed his emblem, the American eagle, which matches well his bold and aspiring spirit. It is impossible to forget that his country and its freely offered hospitality are the very foundation of our national existence, but his services as a scout and soldier have scarcely been valued at their true worth.

THE INDIAN SOLDIER AND SCOUT

The name of Washington is immortal; but who remembers that he was safely guided by a nameless red man through the pathless wilderness to Fort Duquesne? Washington made a successful advance upon the British army at Trenton, on Christmas Eve; but Delaware Indians had reported to him their situation, and made it possible for the great general to hit his enemy hard at an opportune moment. It is a fact that Washington's ability was shown by his confidence in the word of the Indians and in their safe guidance.

In the French and Indian wars there is abundant evidence that both armies depended largely upon the natives, and that when they failed to take the advice of their savage allies they generally met with disaster. This advice was valuable, not only because the Indians knew the country, but because their strategy was of a high order. The reader may have seen at Fort George the statue of Sir William Johnson and King Hendrix, the Mohawk chief. The latter holds in his hand a bundle of sticks. Tradition says that the chief was arguing against the division of their forces to meet the approaching French army, saying: "If we are to fight, we are too few: if we are to die, we are too many!"

As an Indian, and having often heard my people discuss strategic details, I am almost sure that the chief anticipated the tactics of the enemy; and the pathetic sequel is that he was selected to lead a portion of the English forces to Fort Edward that morning, and when only a mile or so out was ambushed by the enemy. He stood his ground, urging his men to face the foe; and when he was shot dead, they were so enraged that with extraordinary valor they routed the French, and thus Hendrix in dying was really the means of saving Forts George and Edward for the colonists.

History says that Braddock was defeated and lost his life at Fort Duquesne because he had neglected and disregarded his Indian scouts, who accordingly left him, and he had no warning of the approach of the foe. Again, the Seminole war in Florida was a failure so long as no Indians were found who were willing to guide the army, and the Government was compelled to make terms, while the swift and overwhelming defeat of the Creeks, a much stronger nation, was due more to the Cherokee and Chickasaw scouts than to the skill of General Jackson. Of course, once the army is guided to an Indian village, and the warriors are surprised in the midst of their women and children, the civilized folk, with superior weapons and generally superior numbers, has every advantage.

The Indian system of scouting has long been recognized as one of the most useful adjuncts of war. His peculiar and efficient methods of communication in the field by means of blanket signals, smoke signals, the arrangement of rock-piles, and by heliograph (small mirrors or reflectors), the last, of course, in more modern days, have all been made use of at one time or another by the United States Army. It is interesting evidence of the world-wide respect for our strategy and methods, that when the Boer commission came to Washington a few years ago, Mr. Vessel called upon me to advise him how he might secure one thousand Sioux and Cheyenne scouts in their war against Great Britain. Of course I told him that it could not be done: that I would not involve my country in an international difficulty. I was similarly approached during the Russo-Japanese war.

The aid of friendly Indians in the case of massacres and surprises of the whites must not be overlooked. It may be recalled that some Cherokee warriors, returning from Washington's later successful expedition against Fort Duquesne, were murdered in their sleep by white frontiersmen after giving them friendly lodging. Here again is brought out the genuine greatness of the Indian character. The Cherokees felt keenly this treacherous outrage by the very people to whom they had just sacrificed the best blood of their young men in their war against the French. Some declared their intention of killing every white man they could find in retaliation for such unprovoked murder; but the chief Ottakullakulla calmly arose and addressed the excited assembly:

"Let us have consideration," said he, "for our white neighbors who are not guilty of this deed. We must not violate our faith or the laws of hospitality by imbruing our hands in the blood of those who are now in our power. They came to us in the confidence of a pledged friendship; let us conduct them safely back within their own confines before we take up the hatchet!"

He carried his point to some extent, and himself saved Captain Stewart, his friend, by giving up all of his property to ransom him. In difficulties between the races since colonial times there has been an unbroken record of heroic work in the rescue of missionaries and other white persons resident among the Indians by their native converts and friends. In the Minnesota Sioux outbreak of 1862 there were many notable instances. A man named Arrow stood beside Mr. Spencer and dared the infuriated warriors to touch him. There were over two hundred white captives saved by friendly Indians and delivered to General Sibley at Camp Release. During the following December some young Yanktonnais Sioux voluntarily ransomed and delivered up two white women and four children. I knew some of these men well; among them Fast Walking, who carried one of the children on his back to safety, after giving his own horse to redeem him. Seldom have such deeds been rewarded or even appreciated. When these men became old and feeble an attempt was made to have them recompensed by Congressional appropriation, but so far as I am informed it has been unsuccessful.

I do not wish to disparage any one, but I do say that the virtues claimed by "Christian civilization" are not peculiar to any culture or religion. My people were very simple and unpractical--the modern obstacle to the fulfilment of the Christ ideal. Their strength lay in self-denial. Not only men, but women of the race have served the nation at most opportune moments in the history of this country.

HISTORIC INDIAN WOMEN

It is remembered that Pocahontas saved the first Virginia colony from utter destruction because of her love for Captain John Smith, who was the heart and brain of the colony. It was the women of the Oneida and Stockbridge Indians who advised their men not to join King Philip against the New England colonies, and, later, pointed out the wisdom of maintaining neutrality during the war of the Revolution.

Perhaps no greater service has been rendered by any Indian girl to the white race than by Catherine, the Ojibway maid, at the height of Pontiac's great conspiracy. Had it not been for her timely warning of her lover, Captain Gladwyn, Fort Detroit would have met the same fate as the other forts, and the large number of Indians who held the siege for three months would have scattered to wipe out the border settlements of Ohio and Pennsylvania. The success of Pontiac would certainly have delayed the settlement of the Ohio valley for many years. It is not to be supposed that Catherine was moved to give her warning by anything save her true womanly instincts. She stood between two races, and in her love and bravery cut short a struggle that might have proved too full of caprice and cruelty on both sides. She was civilization's angel, and should have a niche in history beside Pocahontas.

Sacajawea, the young Indian mother who guided Lewis and Clark in their glorious expedition to the Pacific, was another brave woman. It is true that she was living in captivity, but according to Indian usage that would not affect her social position. It does not appear that she joined the expedition in order to regain her tribe, but rather from a sense of duty and purpose of high usefulness. Not only as guide, but as interpreter, and in rescuing the records of the expedition when their canoe was overturned in the Missouri River, the "Bird Woman" was of invaluable aid, and is a true heroine of the annals of exploration.

THE CHILDREN'S HERO

Nearly all the early explorers owed much to the natives. Who told the white men of the wonders of the Yellowstone Park and the canyon of the Colorado? Who guided them and served them without expectation of credit or honor? It is a principle among us to serve friend or guest to the utmost, and in the old days it was considered ill-bred to ask for any remuneration. To-day we have a new race, the motive of whose actions is the same as that of a civilized man. Nothing is given unless an equivalent is returned, or even a little more if he can secure it. Yet the inherent racial traits are there: latent, no doubt, but still there. The red man still retains his love of service; his love for his country. Once he has pledged his word to defend the American flag, he stands by it manfully.

In the Civil War many Indians fought on both sides, some of them as officers. General Grant had a full-blood Indian on his staff: Col. Ely Parker, afterward Commissioner of Indian Affairs. At one time in recent years a company of Indians was recruited in the regular army, and individual red men are still rendering good service in both army and navy (thirty-five ex-students of Carlisle alone), as well as in other branches of the Federal service. We have lived to see men of our blood in the councils of the nation, and an Indian Register of the Treasury, who must sign all our currency before it is valid. An Indian head is on the five-dollar bill and the new nickel.

George Guess, or Sequoyah, the inventor of the Cherokee alphabet, is the only red man admitted to the nation's Hall of Fame in the Capitol at Washington. The Indian languages, more than fifty in number, are better appreciated and more studied to-day than ever before. Half our states have Indian names, and more than that proportion of our principal lakes and rivers. These names are as richly sonorous as they are packed with significance, and our grandchildren will regret it if we suffer the tongues that gave them birth to die out and be forgotten.

Best of all, perhaps, we are beginning to recognize the Indian's good sense and sanity in the way of simple living and the mastery of the great out of doors. Like him, the wisest Americans are living, playing, and sleeping in the open for at least a part of the year, receiving the vital benefits of the pure air and sunlight. His deeds are carved upon the very rocks; the names he loved to speak are fastened upon the landscape; and he still lives in spirit, silently leading the multitude, for the new generation have taken him for their hero and model.

I call upon the parents of America to give their fullest support to those great organizations, the Boy Scouts and the Camp Fire Girls. The young people of to-day are learning through this movement much of the wisdom of the first American. In the mad rush for wealth we have too long overlooked the foundations of our national welfare. The contribution of the American Indian, though considerable from any point of view, is not to be measured by material acquirement. Its greatest worth is spiritual and philosophical. He will live, not only in the splendor of his past, the poetry of his legends and his art, not only in the interfusion of his blood with yours, and his faithful adherence to the new ideals of American citizenship, but in, the living thought of the nation.

THE END

BIBLIOGRAPHY

The documents chiefly used in the preparation of this book, aside from the author's own observations and personal knowledge, were the annual reports of the United States Commissioner of Indian Affairs, of the United States Board of Indian Commissioners, and of the Bureau of American Ethnology, the proceedings of the Mohonk Indian Conferences, and of religious and philanthropic societies engaged in Indian work; also the reports and magazines published by the larger Indian schools, especially Carlisle and Hampton. The following list of books about the North American Indian is not presented as complete in any sense, but merely as a suggestive guide to the reader who wishes to pursue the subject further:

EARLY STUDENTS AND EXPLORERS

NORTH AMERICAN INDIANS Geo. Catlin

BIOGRAPHY AND HISTORY OF THE INDIANS OF N. A. Drake

WORKS OF John G. Heckewelder

INDIANS OF NORTH AMERICA Henry R. Schoolcraft

THE OREGON TRAIL Parkman

THE JESUITS IN NORTH AMERICA Parkman

JESUIT RELATIONS Edited by Shea

INDIAN MISSIONS

MARY AND I; OR FORTY YEARS AMONG THE SIOUX John Williamson

LIFE OF BISHOP HARE De Wolf Howe

A QUAKER AMONG THE INDIANS T. C. Battey

FATHER JUNIPERO AND THE MISSION INDIANS OF CALIFORNIA H. H.

LEGENDS AND FOLKLORE

BLACKFOOT LODGE TALES G. B. Grinnell

PAWNEE HERO STORIES G. B. Grinnell

ALGONQUIN LEGENDS OF NEW ENGLAND Chas. G. Leland

THE LENAPE AND THEIR LEGENDS Daniel Brinton

THE MAN WHO MARRIED THE MOON AND OTHER PUEBLO FOLK TALES Chas. F. Lummis

MUSIC AND ART

THE INDIANS' BOOK Natalie Curtis

INDIAN BASKETRY George W. James

INDIAN STORY AND SONG Alice C. Fletcher

PRIMITIVE INDIAN MUSIC Frederick Burton

MODERN WRITERS

THE VANISHING RACE Joseph K. Dixon

THE STORY OF THE INDIAN G. B. Grinnell

THE INDIANS OF TO-DAY G. B. Grinnell

NORTH AMERICANS OF YESTERDAY Dellenbaugh

MY FRIEND THE INDIAN James McLaughlin

WHAT THE WHITE MAN MAY LEARN FROM THE INDIAN G. W. James

INDIAN CHIEFS I HAVE KNOWN O. O. Howard

LIVES OF FAMOUS INDIAN CHIEFS N. B. Wood

A CENTURY OF DISHONOR Helen Hunt Jackson (H. H.)

THE INDIAN DISPOSSESSED Setti K. Humphrey

INDIAN SKETCHES Cornelia S. Hulst

EDUCATION OF THE INDIAN (Pamphlet) Hailmann

THE AMERICAN INDIAN Warren K. Moorehead

THE INDIAN IN RELATION TO THE WHITE POPULATION OF THE U. S. (Pamphlet) F. A. McKenzie

FICTION

RAMONA Helen Hunt Jackson

TWO WILDERNESS VOYAGERS F. W. Calkins

THE WOOING OF TOKALA F. W. Calkins

AN INDIAN WINTER J. W. Schultz

CHILDHOOD OF JISHIB THE OJIBWAY A. E. Jenks

THE MIDDLE FIVE Francis La Flesche

THE OJIBWAY James Gilfillan

TABLE OF INDIAN RESERVATIONS IN THE UNITED STATES

(Compiled by the Office of Indian Affairs.)

ARIZONA

Camp McDowell Colorado River Fort Apache Gila Bend Gila River Havasupai Hopi Navajo Papago Salt River San Carlos Walapai

CALIFORNIA

Digger Hupa Valley Mission (28 reserves) Round Valley Tule River Yuma

COLORADO

Ute

IDAHO

Coeur d'Alene Fort Hall Lapwai Lemhi

IOWA

Sauk and Fox

KANSAS

Chippewa and Munsee Iowa Kickapoo Potawatomie Sauk and Fox

MICHIGAN

Isabella L'Anse Ontonagon

MINNESOTA

Bois Fort Deer Creek Fond du Lac Grand Portage Leech Lake Mdewakanton Mille Lac Red Lake Vermillion Lake White Earth White Oak Point and Chippewa

MONTANA

Blackfeet Crow Fort Belknap Fort Peck Jocko Northern Cheyenne

NEBRASKA

Niobrara Omaha Ponca Sioux (additional) Winnebago

NEVADA

Duck Valley Moapa River Pyramid Lake Walker River

NEW MEXICO

Jicarilla Apache Mescalero Apache Pueblos (20 reserves)

NEW YORK

Allegany Cattaraugus Oil Spring Oneida Onondaga St. Regis Tonawanda Tuscarora

NORTH CAROLINA

Qualla Boundary (Cherokee)

NORTH DAKOTA

Devil's Lake Fort Berthold Standing Rock Turtle Mountain

OKLAHOMA

Cherokee Cheyenne and Arapahoe Chickasaw Chocktaw Creek Iowa Kansa or Kaw Kickapoo Kiowa and Comanche Modoc Oakland Osage Otoe Ottawa Pawnee Peoria Ponca Potawatomie Quapaw Sauk and Fox Seminole Seneca Shawnee Wichita Wyandot

OREGON

Grande Ronde Klamath Siletz Umatilla Warm Springs

SOUTH DAKOTA

Crow Creek and Old Winnebago Lake Traverse Cheyenne River Lower Brule Pine Ridge Rosebud Yankton

UTAH

Uintah Valley Uncompahgre

WASHINGTON

Chehalis Columbia Colville Hoh River Lummi Makah Muckleshoot Nisqually Ozette Fort Madison Puyallup Quileute Quinaiette Shoalwater Skokomish Snohomish or Tulalip Spokan Squaxon Island Swinomish Yakima

WISCONSIN

Lac Court Oreille Lac du Flambeau La Pointe Red Cliff Menominee Oneida Stockbridge

WYOMING

Wind River

Charles Eastman

Charles Alexander Eastman (born Hakadah and later named Ohíye S'a; February 19, 1858 – January 8, 1939) was a Santee Dakota physician educated at Boston University, writer, national lecturer, and reformer. In the early 20th century, he was "one of the most prolific authors and speakers on Sioux ethnohistory and American Indian affairs."[1]

Eastman was of Santee Dakota, English and French ancestry. After working as a physician on reservations in South Dakota, he became increasingly active in politics and issues on native American rights, he worked to improve the lives of youths, and founded thirty-two Native American chapters of the Young Men's Christian Association (YMCA). He also helped found the Boy Scouts of America. He is considered the first Native American author to write American history from the Native American point of view.

Early life and education

Eastman was named Hakadah at his birth in Minnesota; his name meant "pitiful last" in Dakota. Eastman was so named because his mother died following his birth. He was the last of five children of Wakantakawin, a mixed-race woman also known as Winona (first born) or Mary Nancy Eastman.[1] She and Eastman's father, a Santee Dakota named Wak-anhdi Ota (Many Lightnings), lived on a Santee Dakota reservation near Redwood Falls, Minnesota.

Winona, meaning first-born daughter in Dakota, was the only child of Seth Eastman, a U.S. Army officer and illustrator, and Wakháŋ Inážiŋ Wiŋ (Stands

Sacred), who married at Fort Snelling in 1830.[1] This post later developed as Minneapolis. Stands Sacred was the fifteen-year-old daughter of Cloud Man, a Santee Dakota chief of French and Mdewakanton descent.[1] Seth Eastman was reassigned from Fort Snelling in 1832, soon after the birth of his daughter Winona (meaning "first-born daughter"). He declared his marriage ended when he left, as was typical of many European-American men in that period. Winona was later called Wakantakawin.

In the Dakota tradition of naming to mark life passages, Hakadah was later named Ohíye S'a (Dakota: "always wins"). He had three older brothers (John, David, and James) and an older sister Mary. During the Dakota War of 1862, Ohíye S'a was separated from his father Wak-anhdi Ota and siblings, and they were thought to have died. His maternal grandmother Stands Sacred (Wakháŋ Inážiŋ Wiŋ) and her family took the boy with them as they fled from the warfare into North Dakota and Manitoba, Canada.[2]

Fifteen years later Ohíyesa was reunited with his father and oldest brother John in South Dakota. The father had converted to Christianity, after which he took the name of Jacob Eastman. John also converted and took the surname Eastman. The Eastman family established a homestead in Dakota Territory. When Ohiyesa accepted Christianity, he took the name Charles Alexander Eastman.

His father strongly supported his sons getting an education in European-American style schools. Eastman and his older brother John attended mission and preparatory schools, and college. Eastman first attended Beloit College and Knox colleges; he graduated from Dartmouth College in 1887. He went on to medical school at Boston University, where he graduated in 1889 and was among the first Native Americans to be certified as a European-style doctor.

His older brother became a minister. Rev. John (Maⓩpiyawaku Kida) Eastman was a Presbyterian missionary at the Santee Dakota settlement of Flandreau, South Dakota.

Career

Charles Eastman worked as an agency physician for the Bureau of Indian

Affairs (BIA) Indian Health Service on the Pine Ridge Reservation and later at the Crow Creek Reservation, both in South Dakota. He cared for Indians after the Wounded Knee massacre. He later established a private medical practice after being forced out of his position, but was not able to make it succeed.

As they were struggling financially, his European-American wife, Elaine Goodale Eastman, encouraged him to write some of the stories of his childhood. At her suggestion (and with her editing help), he published the first two in 1893 and 1894 in St. Nicholas Magazine. It had earlier published poetry of hers.[3] These stories were collected in his first book.

Between 1894–98, Eastman established 32 Indian groups of the Young Men's Christian Association (YMCA), and established leadership programs and outdoor youth camps. In 1899, he helped recruit students for the Carlisle Indian Industrial School in Pennsylvania, which had been established as the first Indian boarding school run by the federal government.

In 1902, Eastman published a memoir, Indian Boyhood, recounting his first fifteen years of life among the Dakota Sioux during the later years of the nineteenth century. In the following two decades, he wrote ten more books, most concerned with his Native American culture. In the early 20th century, he was "one of the most prolific authors and speakers on Sioux ethnohistory and American Indian affairs."[1]

Ruth Ann Alexander, a scholar of his wife Elaine Goodale Eastman, noted that she worked more intensively on Eastman's stories about Indian life than she was given credit. This was a way to share his life and use her literary talents; he published nothing after they separated.[3] Carol Lea Clark viewed their collaboration this way: "together they produced works of a public popularity that neither could produce separately."[2]

Some of Eastman's books were translated into French, German and other European languages, and the books have enjoyed regular reprints. A selection of his writings was published recently as The Essential Charles Eastman (Ohiyesa) (2007).

Inspired by his writings, Ernest Thompson Seton sought Eastman's counsel in forming the Woodcraft Indians, which became a popular group for boys. The

New York YMCA asked both Seton and Eastman to help them design the YMCA Indian Scouts for urban boys, using rooftop gardens and city parks for their activities. In 1910, Seton invited Eastman to work with him and Daniel Carter Beard, of the Sons of Daniel Boone, to found the Boy Scouts of America (BSA).[4] Luther Gulick also consulted with Eastman to assist his developing the Camp Fire Girls with his wife Charlotte.

With his fame as an author and lecturer, Eastman promoted the fledgling Boy Scouts and Camp Fire Girls. He advised them on how to organize their summer camps, and directly managed one of the first Boy Scout camps along the shores of the Chesapeake Bay. His daughter, Irene, worked as a counselor at a Camp Fire Girl camp in Pittsburgh. In 1915, the Eastman family organized its own summer camp at Granite Lake, New Hampshire, where all the family worked for years.[3] Charles served as a BSA national councilman for many years.[4]

National spokesman

In 1911, Eastman was chosen to represent the American Indian at the Universal Races Congress in London.[4] Throughout his speeches and teachings, he emphasized peace and living in harmony with nature.

He was active in national politics, particularly in matters dealing with Indian rights. He served as a lobbyist for the Dakota between 1894 and 1897. In 1903, President Theodore Roosevelt assigned Eastman to help members of the Sioux (Dakota, Nakota, Lakota) to choose English legal names to prevent individuals and families from losing their allotted lands due to confusion over names. Eastman was one of the co-founders of the Society of American Indians (SAI), which pushed for freedom and self-determination for the Indian. From 1923–25, Eastman served as an appointed US Indian inspector under President Calvin Coolidge.

The Calvin Coolidge administration (1923-1929) invited Eastman to the Committee of One Hundred, a reform panel examining federal institutions and activities dealing with Indian nations. This committee recommended that the government conduct an in-depth investigation into reservation life (health, education, economics, justice, civil rights, etc.). This was commissioned through the Department of Interior and conducted by the

Brookings Institution, resulting in the groundbreaking Meriam Report (1928). The findings and recommendations served as the basis of the Franklin D. Roosevelt administration's New Deal for the Indian, which included the 1934 Indian Reorganization Act, encouraging tribes to establish self-government according to constitutional models.

In 1925, the Bureau of Indian Affairs asked Eastman to investigate the death and burial location of Sacagawea, the young woman who guided and interpreted for the Lewis and Clark Expedition in 1805. He determined that she died of old age at the Wind River Indian Reservation in Wyoming on April 9, 1884. More recently, because of newly discovered contemporary records, historians believe that she died in 1812 as a result of an illness following childbirth, at Fort Lisa (North Dakota), in what became North Dakota.[5]

Personal life

In 1891, Eastman married the poet and Indian welfare activist Elaine Goodale, who was serving as Superintendent of Indian Education for the Two Dakotas. She had first taught at Hampton Institute, which then had about 100 Native American students, in addition to African Americans, and at an Indian day school in South Dakota. She supported expanding day schools on reservations for education, rather than sending Native American children away from their families to boarding schools.

The Eastmans had six children together: five daughters and a son. The marriage prospered at first, and Elaine was always interested in Indian issues. Eastman's many jobs, failure to provide financially for the family, and absences on the lecture circuit, put increasing strain on the couple.[3] In 1903, at Elaine's request, they returned to Massachusetts, where the family was based in Amherst.[3]

Charles was traveling extensively, and Elaine Eastman took over managing his public appearances. He lectured about twenty-five times a year across the country. These were productive years for their literary collaboration; he published eight books and she published three. She and Charles separated about 1921, following the death of their daughter Irene in 1918 from influenza during the worldwide epidemic. They never divorced or publicly acknowledged the separation.[3]

Theodore Sargent, a recent biographer of Goodale, noted that Eastman gained acclaim for the nine books he published on Sioux life, whereas Elaine Eastman's seven books received little notice.[6] Others have suggested their differing views on assimilation led to strain. Alexander said the catalyst was a rumor that Eastman had an affair with Henrietta Martindale, a visitor[7] at their camp in 1921 and got her pregnant, after which he and Goodale separated. Although the rumor was said to have been untrue, the couple did not reconcile.[3]

Later life

Charles Eastman built a cabin on the eastern shore of Lake Huron, where he spent his later-year summers. He wintered in Detroit, Michigan with his only son Charles, Jr., also called Ohiyesa. On January 8, 1939 the senior Eastman died from a heart attack in Detroit at age eighty. His interment was at Evergreen Cemetery.

Elaine Goodale Eastman was close to two daughters and families who lived in Massachusetts. Another lived in New Hampshire. Goodale Eastman died in 1953 and was buried in Northampton.[3]

Legacy and honors

As a child, Ohiyesa had learned about herbal medicine from his grandmother. Going to medical school enabled him to draw from both sides of his heritage in becoming a doctor.
1933, Eastman was the first to receive the Indian Achievement Award.[8]
His several books document Sioux Dakota culture at the end of the nineteenth century.
A crater on Mercury was named for him.[9]

Film portrayal

In the HBO film Bury My Heart at Wounded Knee (2007), Eastman was portrayed at different ages by the actors Adam Beach and Chevez Ezaneh.

www.ingramcontent.com/pod-product-compliance
Lightning Source LLC
Chambersburg PA
CBHW062013280526
45787CB00005B/2086